A DICTIONARY OF MANA

INFORMATION AT YOUR FINGERTIPS

Up-to-date and comprehensive, Pitman Dictionaries
are indispensable reference books, providing clear,
crisp explanation of specialist terminology
in an easy-to-use-format

A Concise Dictionary of Accounting and Finance
Accounting Terms Dictionary
Accounting of Economics and Commerce
A Dictionary of Management Terms
A Pocket Dictionary of Business Terms
Business Studies Dictionary
Dictionary of Banking
Dictionary of Banking and Finance
Dictionary of Law
Information Technology Dictionary
Office Practice Dictionary

A Dictionary of Management Terms

R. G. Anderson
FCMA, M Inst AM(Dip), FMS

Pitman Publishing
128 Long Acre, London WC2E 9AN

A Division of Longman Group UK Limited

First published in 1983
Reprinted 1989

© Macdonald & Evans Ltd 1983

British Library Cataloguing in Publication Data
Anderson, R. G.
   A dictionary of management terms.
   1. Management—Dictionaries.
   I. Title.
658′.003′21   HD30.15
ISBN 0 273 03281 X

All rights reserved; no part of this publication may be reproduced, stored in a retrieval system, or transmitted in any form or by any other means, electronic, mechanical, photocopying, recording, or otherwise without either the prior written permission of the Publishers or a licence permitting restricted copying in the United Kingdom issued by the Copyright Licensing Agency, 33–34 Alfred Place, London WC1E 7DP. This book may not be lent, resold, hired out or otherwise disposed of by way of trade in any form of binding or cover other than that in which it is published, without the prior consent of the Publishers.

Printed and bound in Great Britain by
Richard Clay Ltd, Bungay, Suffolk

Preface

The terms outlined in this dictionary are defined in a simple, unambiguous manner so that their meaning is made clear. Included are terms specific to management and those considered essential for the understanding of cost and financial accounting matters, management techniques and business matters of general interest.

The dictionary deals with terms in a practical rather than a theoretical manner and will provide a speedy means of reference for the busy manager wishing to clarify an expression and for management students as a revision aid. It should particularly benefit students studying for the following examinations:

Business Education Council (BEC) regarding various sections relating to management in the examination structure;

The Institute of Administrative Management (IAM) regarding the Diploma in Administrative Management in respect of the subjects "Administrative Management" and "Personnel and Organisational Behaviour";

The Institute of Chartered Secretaries and Administrators (ICSA) in relation to various aspects of "Management Techniques and Services";

The Institute of Management Services (IMS) regarding some aspects of the subject "Organisation";

The Institute of Cost and Management Accountants (ICMA) in respect of the papers "Organisation and Marketing Management" and "Corporate Planning and Control"; and

The Institute of Industrial Managers (IIM) in respect of the subjects "Industrial Management and Organisation" and "Industrial Management Policy and Practice".

Students studying for examinations held by NEBSS, Certificate and Diploma in Management Studies, the Institute of Marketing and the Institute of Personnel Management should also find the book of some use to them.

The entries in the *Dictionary* can also assist college lecturers to develop courses for examinations by providing headings within a subject area, which can then be expanded. Those setting up a business and those already in business will also find the *Dictionary* an invaluable aid when talking to accountants and other specialists.

1983 RGA

Acknowledgments

I gratefully acknowledge permission given by the Institute of Cost and Management Accountants for the use of a number of definitions from their publication *Management Accounting Official Terminology*. I also wish to thank W. D. Scott for the provision of details relating to zero-based administration, to Bob Grice for providing legal aspects of management and to Colin Paul for supplying notes relating to various aspects of management.

I am also indebted to Mrs B. Badger, Lecturer at the Plymouth Business School, Plymouth Polytechnic, for her advice and the provision of additional definitions, the inclusion of which has greatly enhanced the value of the book.

A

Absorbed production overhead. Some costs cannot be specifically identified to units of production as they are incurred for business operations as a whole. This type of cost is classed as overheads and includes indirect materials, indirect wages and indirect expenses. Such costs are charged to products by appropriate overhead absorption methods (methods of recovering overheads) including percentage of direct materials, percentage of direct wages, percentage of prime cost, rate per labour hour or rate per machine hour etc.

Absorption. 1. The integration of one business into the structure of another for purposes of economy of scale, elimination of competition or for other practical reasons. 2. The recovery of fixed and variable overheads by the units produced, or services provided, on the basis of cost recovery techniques such as a rate per machine hour for machine based operations; a rate per labour hour for manually performed operations; as a percentage of direct labour cost or prime cost, etc. Marginal costing does not charge fixed costs to products or services but treats them as period charges to be recovered from total contributions, i.e. the surplus remaining after deducting variable costs from sales income.

ACAS. *See* ADVISORY, CONCILIATION AND ARBITRATION SERVICE.

Accountability. When duties are delegated by a superior to a subordinate, the subordinate assumes responsibility and authority for the performance of such duties and accordingly he is held accountable for their successful achievement. Managers and supervisors should not, however, be held accountable for achieving objectives for which they do not have authority. *See* PRINCIPLE OF CORRESPONDENCE.

Accountant. An accountant may be defined as a person having responsibility for the custodianship of a company's assets; for ensuring that statutory records are maintained and that business transactions are recorded in proper books of account; and ensuring that accounting conventions, principles and practices are adhered to. Of course, this is a broad definition and it is necessary to distinguish between two different classes of accountant, i.e. financial accountant (q.v.) and management accountant (q.v.).

Accounting. The activities performed by an accountant with regard to business transactions are referred to as accounting. They relate to the recording of sales, purchases, stock movements, calculation of wages and salaries, making payments to suppliers and preparing profit and loss accounts and balance sheets, etc. The accounting activities of a business are extremely diverse embracing not only normal bookkeeping but planning and control activities relating to budgetary control, cash flow analysis and the periodic preparation of operating statements and control reports. *See* MANAGEMENT ACCOUNTING.

Accounting period. The normal accounting period for a business embraces a complete financial year at the end of which it is necessary to prepare statutory returns for employee taxation, VAT schedules, profit and loss accounts (q.v.) and balance sheets (q.v.). Most businesses operate some form of budgetary control system (q.v.) which is concerned with the preparation of monthly operating statements so that control can be maintained over all business operations in the short, rather than the long, term. The monthly accounting activities are performed in what are known as accounting periods or budget periods. *See* BUDGET CONTROL PERIOD.

Acid test. This is the measure of the financial solvency of a business regarding its capability of meeting its current liabilities. It is also referred to as the liquidity ratio or liquid asset ratio. The liquidity ratio (q.v.) is computed by comparing those current assets which can be quickly converted into cash, or which are already in this form, with the amounts owing (current liabilities) which must be cleared in the current period.

$$\text{Liquidity ratio} = \frac{\text{Debtors + bank cash + cash in hand}}{\text{Total current liabilities}}$$

The ratio should be at least 1:1 indicating that the level of liquidity is sufficient to meet the current liabilities. *See* CURRENT LIABILITIES.

Action learning. *See* MANAGEMENT TRAINING TECHNIQUES.

Activity sampling. A technique for sampling work activities, instead of continuous observations, as a means of achieving economy in the time spent collecting facts relating to each of the activities under consideration. It enables data to be obtained indicating whether persons or machines are working or not working, whether the telephone is being used or not and whether a person is in the office or not and so on. It is possible to assess the use of resources and the level of productivity by this means. The technique is based on the law of averages and observations are made at random time intervals to avoid bias. The time intervals may be established from random number tables or by selecting numbers from a hat, i.e. by pure chance.

Actual observation. *See* EXPONENTIAL SMOOTHING.

Adaptive (dynamic) system. An adaptive system is a system, such as a business organisation, which behaves dynamically as it responds to changing circumstances caused by random influences in its operating environment. These influences include inflation, fluctuations in demand, shortages of raw materials, bad weather, government legislation and industrial action, etc. It is a self-organising system which modifies its inputs as a result of measuring its outputs and compares them with its control parameters in an attempt to optimise its performance.

Added value. This is a recently introduced method which is being used to replace profit sharing plans. The added value is the balance of the company income after costs of material and services have been deducted. The added value is shared out between (*a*) the company for fixed expenses such as rent, rates, depreciation, interest payments and profits, and (*b*) the employees for wages, salaries and pension schemes. All employees are encouraged to participate to enhance the added value by increased shop floor productivity, improved management techniques, elimination of wasteful practices and better sales and marketing. *See* VALUE ADDED.

Administration. The activity concerned with the smooth functioning of business activities achieved by means of well-designed administrative systems supported by effective management. The administration of a business is entrusted to the board of directors (partners or proprietors) which is the governing body. The board may be known collectively as "the administration" of the business. Office managers are also known as administrators; therefore, all managers may be defined as administrative managers responsible for administering the affairs of the business. They are responsible for planning and controlling all business operations to achieve defined objectives.

Administration cost budget. A financial and/or quantitative statement prepared for a defined period of time outlining the various costs expected to be incurred for a defined set of operating circumstances, e.g. levels of activity, number of personnel employed, volume of paper work to be processed, etc. Each administrative department including accounting, stock control, payroll, purchasing, sales invoicing and sales ledger, production planning and data processing, etc. prepares a cost budget. The annual budgeted overheads may be allocated to months and charged as period costs to the budgeted profit and loss account. The overheads may be absorbed by units produced on a suitable basis such as a percentage of factory cost or they may not be absorbed at all but form part of fixed overheads (q.v.) to be met from contributions (q.v.).

Administrative management. See ADMINISTRATION, ORGANISATION THEORY 2 and PIONEERS OF MANAGEMENT.

Administrative management, Institute of. IAM was founded in 1915 and has a membership in the region of 10,000. It promotes administrative management in commerce, industry, central and local government and offers its own professional qualifications in the form of the Certificate and Diploma in Administrative Management. Its examinations are held twice a year at various centres at home and abroad. Many colleges offer tuition for the examinations. It produces standard works of reference relating to periodical surveys which includes Office Salaries Analysis and Office Job Evaluation, etc. It also publishes a monthly journal the *British Journal of Administrative Management.*

Advisory, Conciliation and Arbitration Service (ACAS). A body which came into existence partly from the conciliation services of the Department of Employment. ACAS is an independent body formed as a result of the Employment Protection Act 1975 and has a duty to promote the improvement of industrial relations and to encourage collective bargaining (q.v.). It provides advisory services to employers, unions and to individual employees. ACAS often performs conciliatory duties relating to matters which may have been referred to industrial tribunals and arbitrates between employers and unions when disputes occur.

Agent. A person with authority to represent a principal in making contractual agreements with third parties. Under the Partnership Act 1890 a partner is an agent of the firm and of each of his partners for the purposes of the business partnership and all partners have authority to bind the others. In respect of a public company contracts are made by directors on its behalf in which case they are acting as agents.

Amalgamation. The result of a merger. It is a combination of two or more business entities into one business organisation.

Appraisal. The process of reviewing an individual's performance and progress in a job and assessing his potential for future promotion. It is a systematic method of obtaining, analysing and recording information about a person. There are three main groups of performance review activities. 1. *Performance reviews* which relate to the need to improve the performance of individuals and thereby improve the effectiveness of the organisation as a whole. 2. *Potential reviews* which attempt to deal with the problem of predicting the level and type of work that the individual will be capable of doing in future. 3. *Reward reviews* which relate to the distribution of such rewards as pay, power and status. *See* MANAGEMENT BY OBJECTIVES, MERIT RATING, PERFORMANCE STANDARDS and SELECTION TESTS.

Aptitude tests. *See* SELECTION TESTS.

Arbitration. The referral of a dispute to a mutually acceptable referee (arbitrator) for its settlement with predetermined agreement to accept the arbitrator's decision.

Articles of Association. A document which outlines the regulations for the management of a company. A company limited by shares usually files its own articles but a model set applies to companies who do not register their own articles. The Articles of Association include matters relating to share capital; election of directors, powers and duties; dividends; transfer of shares, meetings, accounts and audit, etc. *See* MEMORANDUM OF ASSOCIATION.

Asset. Business assets are resources or items of value owned by the business and which are utilised in the normal course of business operations to produce goods for sale in order to yield a profit. Assets may be classified as either fixed, current, tangible or intangible. 1. Fixed assets (q.v.) include land and buildings, plant and machinery which normally have an intrinsic value. 2. Current assets (q.v.) include stocks, work in process, debtors, cash at bank and in hand as well as repayments such as insurance premiums paid in advance. 3. Tangible assets (q.v.) are those items of substance owned by a business. 4. Intangible assets (q.v.) relate to goodwill and trademarks which do not have an intrinsic value but are often of significance to the profitability of a business.

Asset replacement. The replacement of fixed assets (q.v.), particularly plant and machinery, is essential when the existing assets are worn out as new machines are necessary to maintain the level of productivity. In other instances, perfectly good machines may need to be replaced by high technology machines for the purpose of improving business administrative efficiency by the use of computers and for improving production efficiency by the use of automated processes. *See* AUTOMATION and PLANT REPLACEMENT STRATEGY.

Asset stripping. The purchase of an unprofitable business for the purpose of disposing of its assets on a piecemeal basis rather than as a going concern in order to realise a profit.

Asset utilisation ratio. A measure of the extent to which assets are utilised in relation to the value of the sales. Operating assets must be utilised as fully as possible in order to optimise the investment in plant and machinery and working capital. A low utilisation factor may indicate a surplus of assets in relation to the level of sales achieved. A high utilisation factor indicates that they are being used effectively. It may also indicate that additional investment in fixed assets is necessary if sales trends are increasing beyond the present production capacity. Two methods of measurement may be used:

1. Turnover of assets = $\dfrac{\text{Sales value}}{\text{Total operating assets}}$

e.g. $\dfrac{£100,000}{£80,000} = 1.25$ times

2. £ of assets per £ of sales = $\dfrac{\text{Operating assets}}{\text{Sales value}}$

e.g. $\dfrac{£80,000}{£100,000} = £.8^*$

*Note that £.8 indicates that £800 of assets generate £1,000 of sales.

Associated company. Companies associated through mutual trade interests whereby one company may have a minority shareholding in other companies to enhance trading operations to the mutual benefit of all the companies.

Attainment tests. *See* SELECTION TESTS.

Audit, management. *See* MANAGEMENT AUDIT.

Auditor. There are two categories of auditor: internal and external. 1. Internal auditors are employees of the company and are responsible for performing impartial monitoring activities. They review accounting and other procedures and systems as the basis of a service to management. Auditors act in an advisory capacity and are not answerable to functional managers. Their position in the organisation enables them to report to the highest level of management above the functional level. This eliminates functional friction and bias. Audit reports are presented to the level of management able to implement acceptable recommendations. 2. External auditors are not employees of the company and they usually inspect accounts and business records at the end of the financial year to ensure that they present a true and fair view of profits, losses, assets and liabilities.

Audit packages. A preprepared program which assists the auditing of computer systems. They often provide facilities for extracting records randomly from master files so that they may be printed out for inspection.

Authorised capital. The authorised share capital of a public limited company is stated in the Memorandum of Association (q.v.). It is also known as nominal capital. It is not necessary to issue the whole of the authorised capital when a company is first formed as it is normal practice to call up the amount of share capital needed to commence operations and then call up further capital from the shareholders to finance expansion or working capital requirements as required.

Authority. An executive/subordinate relationship in a working environment whereby superiors are able to give instructions to subordinates to perform specific activities and achieve defined objectives. Authority, therefore, provides the basis for getting things done in an organisation. Executive/subordinate relationships are known as line relationships. It is, however, necessary to stipulate the limits of an individual's authority.

Autocratic management style. A management style whereby a manager defines his plans and gives commands without prior consultation with subordinates. This, of course, is the opposite management style to the more generally acceptable democratic approach which provides for consultation with subordinates. Autocratic management is a feature of authoritarian organisation which practises a dictatorial philosophy, expecting orders to be executed without question and without expectation of initiative from subordinates. It does not engender motivation to achieve goals, but assumes people like to be told what they are to do because they do not wish to take on responsibility. *See* MANAGEMENT STYLE.

Automated decisions. Automated decisions are a feature of automated processes which have in-built decision-making facilities for such requirements as opening or closing valves or adjusting the depth of cut on a cylinder block during a metal cutting process. In the administrative sector of an organisation, a computer program may contain instructions for testing the status of the system and effect conditional branching to a routine to deal with abnormal situations such as automatic reordering of stocks which have fallen to a predefined reorder level. Such decisions are possible for problems of a structured nature, i.e. when they accord to standardised rules which enables algorithms to be determined for their solution. *See* STRUCTURED DECISIONS.

Automation. A term sometimes used to describe the mechanisation of industrial and administrative processes and operations. The term relates to the use of machines instead of people in pursuit of higher productivity. More precisely, automation is the mechanisation of processes which have inbuilt capability for modifying their behaviour, when relevant, by the use of sensors and control mechanisms, in order to achieve specified requirements as indicated by control parameters. An automated process, therefore, is a mechanised activity with inbuilt control for adjusting its behaviour on the basis of feedback which classifies such a system as an adaptive or dynamic system (q.v.). Automated production flowlines in the factory are widely used in the processing of foodstuffs and chemicals and for assembly lines. In the office, the administrative processing area, computers are used for producing business documents automatically and performing other accounting and control routines such as production planning and control, budgetary and cost control, automatic stock reordering and so on. Strictly, this is sophisticated mechanisation but in common usage goes under the heading of automation. It all depends upon the degree of intelligence or information processing and decision-making attributes built into the system and the extent it can function without human intervention. The elements of automation have been described as "the three Cs", i.e. communication, computation and control. *See also* MECHANISATION.

Autonomous. Autonomous operations are conducted without recourse to or influence from other sources on a go-it-alone basis of self-sufficiency in the management and control of a business entity. An example is the managing director of a branch works who plans and controls its activities on a day-to-day basis without interference from head office. Operations would usually be conducted within the framework of overall corporate policy so co-operation and coordination between head and branch offices is essential when annual targets, policies and objectives are being established. Autonomy provides the foundations for a common aim to be pursued throughout a business regardless of its geographical dispersion, but without the stifling influences of tight control from above. Local management has the prosperity of the business in its own hands. This approach to business management encourages motivation and flexibility and is evidence of a greater acceptance of innovation, adaptability and accountability.

B

Balance sheet. This is a summary of a company's assets (q.v.) and liabilities, including share capital (q.v.) and reserves, as at a defined moment in time. It provides a snapshot of the state of the business financially and it is essential that it portrays a true and fair view of the status of the business as a going concern (q.v.). It is usually prepared historically after the conclusion of an accounting period (q.v.) or at the year-end. Historical values are often used whereby the fixed assets are recorded at cost less depreciation and current assets at the lower of cost or market value for such items as raw materials and component parts. In some instances, however, it is financially prudent to evaluate assets at current replacement values in order to assess a more accurate value of the business on a present worth basis. *See also* CURRENT LIABILITIES, CAPITAL RESERVE, REVENUE RESERVE, ASSET and PLANT REPLACEMENT STRATEGY.

Bankruptcy. It is interesting to note that bankruptcy cannot apply to limited companies, but only individuals. The term applies to the inability of persons to meet their financial commitments. Legal proceedings are undertaken for the purpose of securing a person's assets to provide funds to pay wholly, or in part, the amounts owed to creditors. When discharged from bankruptcy, persons can recommence business without the problem of the former debts. The proceedings in relation to a company are referred to as liquidation (q.v.).

Bar chart. A type of chart used for presenting control information to management. Data relating to costs, production or sales can be plotted by time period as a series of bars, the length of each bar depending upon the value of the data represented. By means of the varying lengths of bar, values can be discerned and compared at a glance. A well-known example of a bar chart is the Gantt chart.

Bayes' rule. This rule states that when deciding between two or more alternative choices the alternative with the highest expectation should be selected. This requires the assessment of all alternative expectations which can be recorded in a pay-off table. *See* DECISION THEORY, EXPECTATION and MAXIMUM LIKELIHOOD RULE.

Behavioural sciences. These include the study of sociology and psychology. A knowledge of the behavioural sciences is particularly useful to managers as it will aid their analysis of behaviour within their organisation. Behavioural scientists have developed many techniques of use in work organisations which can be broadly classified into three categories: (*a*) tools for diagnosing problem areas; (*b*) training methods and programmes; (*c*) facilitation of organisational change and development (q.v.).

Black box. A concept which allows the operation of a system to be understood in general terms, without the complication of technical detail. Therefore, an entity whose *modus operandi* is an unknown factor is referred to as a black box. The term is often used in relation to the electronic computer on the premise that the manner of its internal operation is a mystery to everyone except electronic experts. It is unnecessary for the layman, manager or even a computer user to understand the workings of a computer in detail as long as its inputs and outputs are fully understood. In the early days of computers, auditors were confronted with the task of auditing computer based systems but they did not understand the working of them and so audited "round" the computer, not through it, treating the computer as a black box. Nowadays, auditors are more knowledgeable about such matters and now audit "through" the computer taking account of what happens to data in the computer after it has been input prior to being output.

Black labour market. *See* MOONLIGHTING.

Blue chip. The term is used to describe the ordinary shares of companies of repute, which are nationally and internationally known, and which are regarded by the stock market and the public as being financially sound and provide a relatively safe investment.

Board of directors. This is a collective term describing the management committee of a company made up of the directors. *See also* MANAGEMENT.

Brainstorming. A technique applied to problem solving by evaluating ideas put forward by a group of people convened specially for the purpose. It is an application of the principle that several heads are better than one with problems being viewed from several points of view. An accountant, no doubt, will attempt to view problems from a financial point of view whereas an engineer will view a system as a series of interconnected sub-systems structurally linked on a coordinated basis to achieve specific functions. *See also* THINKTANK.

Break-even analysis. *See* BREAK-EVEN CHART and BREAK-EVEN POINT.

Break-even chart. A graphical presentation of fixed costs, variable costs and sales income for various sets of circumstances, i.e. level of costs and volume of sales. It illustrates the profits or losses incurred at different levels of activity, the break-even point (q.v.) and the margin of safety (q.v.).

Break-even point. The point when sales income equates to total cost, i.e. the level of activity when neither profit or loss is made. It may be computed on the basis of units or sales as follows:

1. Break-even units = $\dfrac{\text{Fixed overhead}}{\text{Contribution per unit}}$

2. Break-even sales value = $\dfrac{\text{Fixed overhead}}{\text{Contribution to sales ratio}}$

See CONTRIBUTION and FIXED OVERHEADS.

Break-up value. When a company fails and cannot be sold as a going concern (q.v.), its assets are sold as separate lots, sometimes by auction, for whatever amount can be realised in order to minimise the total loss.

Bridlington Agreement. Drawn up in 1939 by the TUC it sets out to minimise the likelihood of disputes between unions, particularly those resulting from union competition. The principles on which the agreement was based were geared toward unions entering into agreement with others with whom they were in frequent contact in order to establish their position over spheres of influence, recognition, transfers, and so on.

British Institute of Management (BIM). Formed in 1947 to promote high standards of managerial professionalism and practice within the United Kingdom and to project increased understanding of the importance of the managerial role in the conduct of business operations. BIM branches organise meetings on topics of interest to members most of whom are practising managers. Some members are lecturers in management subjects having previously been in managerial posts. The official journal of the BIM is *Management Today*.

British Standards Institution (BSI). The national institution for the preparation of British standards relating to such aspects as standard dimensions of screw threads, electrical standards, methods of testing, codes of practice, terms, definitions and symbols for flowcharting, etc. BSI represents the UK in international organisations concerned with the preparation of international standards.

Broker. Brokers are agents acting as intermediaries between buyers and sellers, for which they receive a commission, called brokerage, which is usually calculated as a percentage of the value of the transaction. There are many different types of broker such as insurance broker, stock broker and others dealing with specific commodities.

"Buck stops here, The". A colloquial expression which means the end of the road has been reached as far as passing the buck (q.v.) is concerned. There is no one else in the management hierarchy to delegate to. *See* DELEGATION.

Budget. A budget may be defined as a financial and/or quantitative statement, prepared and approved prior to a defined period of time, of the policy to be pursued during that period for the purpose of attaining a given objective. It may include income, expenditure and the employment of capital. Distinction should be made between a budget and a forecast. A budget is not in itself a forecast but is a planned course of action based on a forecast of a future situation. *See also* FUNCTIONAL BUDGET, MASTER BUDGET, SUBSIDIARY BUDGET and DEMAND FORECASTING.

Budgetary control. The ICMA define budgetary control as follows:

"The establishment of budgets relating the responsibilities of executives to the requirements of a policy, and the continuous comparison of actual with budgeted results, either to secure by individual action the objective of that policy or to provide a basis for its revision."

The definition clearly indicates that it is a means of pinpointing responsibility and accountability of specific executives for the achievement of specified objectives which is the basis of responsibility accounting. *See also* ACCOUNTABILITY and PRINCIPLE OF RESPONSIBILITY.

Budget centre. A budget centre may be defined as a section of an organisation for which separate budgets can be compiled as a basis for control. Budget centres are often based on the functional organisation of a business which allows budgets to be prepared for departments, sections and individuals as the need arises. Budget centres pinpoint accountability very positively.

Budget committee. A committee established for the formulation of budget policy, planning and administration of budgetary control procedures. The committee is often chaired by the chief executive and consists of senior managers of the various functions within the company, including the budget officer (q.v.) and accountant (q.v.).

Budget control period. Budgets are structured on the basis of short term control periods. Some factors are controlled on a daily basis such as overtime, absenteeism and production rejects. Other aspects are controlled on a weekly or monthly basis. It is essential for managers responsible for achieving budget objectives to be aware of the actual results being achieved in sufficient time to enable effective control action to be taken, particularly to remedy adverse situations. *See also* CONTROL.

Budget cost allowance. Budget cost allowance may be defined as the cost which a budget centre is expected to incur in a budget control period (q.v.). This usually comprises variable costs (q.v.) in direct proportion to the volume of production or service achieved and fixed costs as a proportion of the annual budget.

Budget draft. An initial budget presented to the budget committee (q.v.) for consideration and approval. Such drafts are seldom accepted at their initial presentation due to such aspects as insufficient profit, inadequate return on capital employed (q.v.) or inadequate turnover of assets in relation to sales. Modifications are made as requested by the committee after consultation with management and are then resubmitted for further consideration until they are finally approved for implementation.

Budget factor. *See* LIMITING FACTOR.

Budget officer. The administrative activities of the budget committee are the responsibility of a budget officer who is usually a member of the management accountant's staff. His duties include interpreting the policy of the budget committee and the dissemination of outline plans to executives, providing them with the bases for formulating budgets within the framework of policy for their area of responsibility and accountability. He is responsible for coordinating all the functional budgets (q.v.) and subsidiary budgets (q.v.) as a basis for constructing the master budget (q.v.).

Budget structure. The structure of the financial accounting system is normally used as the framework for structuring functional budgets to facilitate the preparation of budget control statements. These statements provide for the direct comparison of budgeted and actual results which provides management with details of operating variances as a basis for control.

Bulletin. *See* INFORMATION TECHNOLOGY.

Business cycle. This cycle is the variations, the peaks and troughs, which occur in business operations as fluctuations in the level of production, supply and sales. On occasions this is due to seasonal variations. In other cases, business activity varies as a result of stop go policies of the government to ward off the threat of inflation and increasing interest rates, etc. Booms and slumps also occur as a result of natural economic forces which tend to occur cyclically. Business planning attempts to foresee such events, which are threats to the smooth operation of the business or even to its survival, and to apply corrective measures to minimise the effect of such events.

Business forecasting. *See* DEMAND FORECASTING.

Business game. The activity which simulates business operations for the purpose of evaluating the results of decisions made by the different participants. The participants act as competitors and the outcome of the decisions made by them are often influenced by the decisions of competitors. In this way, the results of varying cost structures, selling prices and stock levels can be assessed. The purpose of business games is to provide both a stimulating means of training executives and for assessing business strategy. The rules of the game are incorporated into computer programs. During the course of the game the computer keeps control of the proceedings and informs competitors of the results of their actions. *See* MANAGEMENT TRAINING TECHNIQUES.

Business information. *See* MANAGEMENT INFORMATION SYSTEM.

Business model. A business model is a symbolic representation of a real-life system. Models are constructed on the basis of constraints, relationships and variables which are assembled in algebraic or algorithmic form, e.g. profit is equal to sales income less total costs, i.e.

$$P = S - C.$$

Models can be run on a computer by means of specially prepared programs and this enables the operation to be simulated. A number of years' operations can be processed in this way in a very short time depending upon the complexity of the model. By modifying the value of specific variables it is possible to assess the "What if?" situation, thus indicating to management what would happen if specific conditions existed in the real system. They are then able to choose the best strategy to optimise system performance. Modelling packages (q.v.) for use with a computer are available. The use of models avoids the need to make physical changes to a system on a trial and error basis thereby avoiding the costs and time constraints of such a course of action. Of course, a model is only as good as its construction: if it omits specific relationships, constraints or variables then it will fail to represent the true real-life system and it would be dangerous to implement change on the basis of such a model. The results obtained from running the model will not represent the true operation of the system and are accordingly worthless. It is possible to construct models very accurately but assign inaccurate values to the variables which prevents accurate results from being obtained. With regard to stock control a model may be compiled perhaps for the purpose of optimising the investment in stocks. Variations in the time it takes for supplies to be received (lead time, q.v.) and usage rates may be established from historical information and applied to the model, progressively changing the variables one at a time to assess the outcome in each case. Information will be derived regarding the number of times (frequency) items are out of stock, the number of times the maximum stock has been exceeded and the effect of changes in safety stock levels (q.v.), reorder levels (q.v.), order quantities and usage rates.

Business policy. *See* COMPANY POLICY

C

Capability profile. The strengths and weaknesses of a business, established from an assessment of corporate capability, may be summarised to form a capability profile in which a number of factors are recorded. The factors may be recorded under such headings as men (human resources), machines (mechanised (capital) resources), money (financial resources), markets (sales outlets) and management (business control). The profile enables management to discern where the company's relative strengths and weaknesses lie and to take effective action to eliminate weaknesses and take advantage of relative strengths. A business may be weak with regard to its production resources as the machines in use are technologically obsolete or worn out. The financial strength of the business may be inadequate perhaps requiring an influx of additional capital from the uncalled capital available from shareholders, or product life cycles may be at the lowest peak requiring to be replaced with a new or revamped range of products in order to maintain, or increase, market share. *See also* CORPORATE APPRAISAL and PRODUCT LIFE ANALYSIS.

Capacity. *See* PRODUCTION CAPACITY.

Capacity ratio. This has been defined as the actual number of direct working hours divided by (or expressed as a percentage of) the budgeted number of standard hours. The ratio may be calculated in the following way:

$$\text{Capacity ratio} = \frac{\text{Actual hours worked on production}}{\text{Budgeted standard hours}} \times \frac{100}{1}$$

The ratio is a measure of the extent to which planned capacity has been utilised. Variations can be investigated and a reduction in the use of capacity may be caused by machine breakdown or power failure causing idle time. Appropriate action may then be taken within the sphere of influence of a specific supervisor or manager. A power failure is, of course, not within the sphere of influence of internal personnel.

Capital. In general, capital may be defined as the value of assets (wealth) owned by a business and which are used during the course of business operations to generate additional capital or wealth. When a business first comes into existence the initial capital may be provided by the proprietor(s) from savings or by means of a loan from friends or the bank. The capital is then called loan capital. The initial influx of capital will normally be in the form of cash which needs to be converted into plant and machinery, buildings and stocks of materials prior to commencing operations. The initial capital, therefore, is converted into other forms of assets for pursuing the purpose and objectives of the business. The machines will be used to convert materials into saleable products which will generate funds for further purchases of materials and the replacement or addition to machines to facilitate expansion. A surplus of income over expenditure is known as profit and may be used for self-financing business expansion. This increases the proprietor's capital. On the other hand, a deficit, i.e. a shortfall of income in relation to expenditure, is a loss which reduces the amount of the proprietor's capital invested in the business. Capital is also reduced by cash withdrawals. If a business is formed by a partnership the capital is usually provided by each of the partners in agreed proportions. The capital of a limited company is provided by the shareholders who may be ordinary or preference shareholders. The ordinary shareholder's capital is referred to as equity capital (q.v.). Revenue reserves derived from retained profits belong to the ordinary shareholders. The preference shareholders are paid a fixed dividend on their shareholding.

Capital budgeting. The term relates to the evaluation of several alternative capital projects for the purpose of assessing those which have the highest rate of return on investment. Various methods are used for evaluation, e.g. ranking by inspection, pay-back period (*see* PAY-BACK METHOD), proceeds per £ of capital outlay, average annual proceeds per £ of capital outlay, average income derived from the book value of the investment, net present value and yield, etc. *See also* INVESTMENT APPRAISAL, NET WORTH and YIELD OF INVESTMENT.

Capital employed. The initial capital for a business in the form of cash will be converted into assets for commencing business operations. It is, therefore, important to distinguish between the capital employed in a business which relates to the source of funds, i.e. funds provided by the proprietor, partner or shareholders, and the employment of the capital which relates to the way in which the funds are used, i.e. their disposition. The capital employed in a business is also equal to the net worth of a business. *See* CAPITAL, NET WORTH and RETURN ON CAPITAL EMPLOYED.

Capital expenditure control. Capital expenditure projects are normally initiated either by an executive director, general or departmental manager or the board of directors. All but the smallest projects must be formally presented to the board for approval. It is essential for the board to assess whether capital expenditure proposals accord with the framework of future plans, which may include the initiation of an extensive modernisation programme in the near future. Each submission should be subjected to a detailed economic study (cost/benefit appraisal q.v.) to assess the anticipated yield on the investment which may be calculated as follows:

$$\text{Yield on investment} = \frac{\text{Reduction in annual operating costs (excluding depreciation)}}{\text{Capital expenditure (investment)}} \times 100$$

When a number of projects are competing for scarce funds then it is necessary to select the most suitable projects which, on a purely economic basis, would be on the basis of yield on investment (q.v.).

Capital reserve. A capital reserve can arise from a revaluation of assets over and above their current book value in order to represent current valuations as a result of inflation. The excess of the revaluation constitutes a capital reserve. This arises in respect of land and buildings in particular, which tend to appreciate rather than depreciate. If revaluations are not implemented asset values will be understated which could make a business prone to takeover bids. *See* FIXED ASSETS.

Case studies. *See* MANAGEMENT TRAINING TECHNIQUES.

Cash budget. A budget which incorporates the cash flow element of other budgets relative to production costs, administration costs and marketing costs, etc. It is of great importance to a business to ensure that cash resources are sufficient to meet commitments in each operating period. Assessing the inward and outward cash flows for each operating period provides the basis for this. When cash shortfalls are indicated, sufficient time is available to negotiate bank loans or overdrafts. When cash surpluses are envisaged arrangements can be made to utilise such cash profitably by short-term investments. There are three methods of cash budgeting—receipts and payments method, adjusted profit and loss account method and source and disposition of funds statement (also known as balance sheet method). *See* CASH FLOW.

Cash flow. Cash flow is the lifeblood of a business (providing it is flowing inwards more than it is flowing outwards) for cash deficiencies can cause critical situations such as failure to meet current liabilities (tax payments, wages and amounts due to trade creditors). Profits may be good on paper but unless sales are converted into cash, business operations will come to a standstill and the business may have to go into liquidation unless a life saving exercise can be instigated. In order to ensure cash flows are adequate the investment in stocks should be controlled as well as amounts owing by customers. *See* CASH BUDGET, PAPER PROFIT and also STOCK CONTROL.

Ceefax. *See* TELETEXT.

Centralisation. A philosophy which affects the way in which many different facets of business are organised. Centralisation can relate to the grouping of services such as purchasing, reprographics, typing and data processing as well as management services in order to achieve economy of scale. Management control may also be centralised in relation to group operations in order to coordinate diverse and dispersed activities. *See* DECENTRALISATION.

Centre for Interfirm Comparison. *See* INTERFIRM COMPARISON.

Chain of command. The formal superior/subordinate relationships which exist in a business organisation structure. Superiors communicate instructions (commands) down through the organisation via the various levels of management (subordinates), and receive feedback (information) relating to the status of operations which provides the intelligence with which to modify courses of action (decisions) to achieve the aims of the business (objectives). The Scalar Principle, attributed to Henri Fayol, requires that a clear line of formal authority be indicated running from the top to the bottom of the organisation, i.e. from the chief executive to the operating personnel. The line of formal authority is based on the principle of unity of command which means that each subordinate is responsible to only one superior.

Chief executive. *See* MANAGING DIRECTOR.

Closed loop system. A term used in the context of control systems both of an organisational and electronic nature. It is a system which measures its outputs by a sensor and communicates this data to a comparator (q.v.) by the process of feedback. It is a system for measuring deviations from planned performance enabling it to modify its input of resources so that the desired state of the system, i.e. a specified output (objective) can be achieved. Managerial control systems are of the closed loop type as they generally compare what should have happened to what has happened. The differences are noted and those of significance indicate that action is required to rectify the situation on the basis of management by exception (q.v.). Many closed loop systems are self-regulating as they contain built-in control mechanisms, examples being the Watt governor which regulates the speed of an engine; and the thermostat in a heating system which regulates the temperature of the water. *See also* EXCEPTION REPORTING.

Closed shop. The limitation of employment in a business to employees who are members of a specific trade union.

Collective bargaining. Discussions and negotiations between employers and employees, *via* their trade union representatives, for establishing agreements relating to specific groups of employees regarding wage rates, working conditions, hours of work, redundancy, holidays and so on. *See* INCOMES POLICIES.

Commercial director. An official of a company having responsibility for administering its commercial activities. In general, the duties of a commercial director (or manager) may include negotiating contracts, control of purchasing and stocks, transportation and warehouse, cost estimating and shipping, etc. The precise nature of these activities will vary from one company to another, depending on purpose and structure.

Committee. A group of persons formed for a stated purpose which may be a standing committee or one convened for a special purpose. Some committees are for special investigative requirements of the government; others are for internal policy formulation. (The board of directors is a committee for this purpose.) There are also works committees dealing with general administrative matters, data processing steering committees, and those relating to health and safety, cost reduction, quality and budgetary control, etc.

Communication. Communication in business is paramount to its success. It may be defined as the process of imparting information from one person to another, or from one process to another in automated systems. Information is the lifeblood of a business but it is useless unless communicated by the correct source to the correct destination by the most efficient means. Essential decisions will otherwise fail to be made either due to not being received in time, or being received by the wrong person who will take no action. Many businesses have networks of interlinked computers for the speedy interchange of data which speeds up the flow of information. Other types of business have systems which provide for the speedy input of data as events occur, in order to provide instant responses for conveying information, for example airline seat reservations, hotel accommodation and holiday enquiries.

Company. A company may be defined as a group of persons formed for carrying on business or trading activities. Companies are controlled by the Companies Act 1948 as amended and expanded by the Companies Acts 1967, 1976, 1980 and 1981 and by s. 9 of the European Communities Act 1972. 1. A public company has a separate identity to its members and is not managed by its owners, i.e. the shareholders. The powers of management are delegated to a board of directors elected in accordance with the Articles of Association (q.v.). 2. As a result of the 1980 Companies Act, a company is private unless it is registered as a public company. A private company cannot invite the public to buy its shares. 3. Registered companies are usually limited, i.e. the liability of its shareholders is limited to the amount of capital they have agreed to subscribe. The Acts also provide for unlimited companies but members are personally responsible for the debts of the company. *See* LIMITED LIABILITY and UNLIMITED LIABILITY.

Company policy. Company policy outlines the philosophy underlying a company's actions which determine the ethical, sociological and economic framework in which it functions. Such policy determines the company image to the various social groups including employees, customers, suppliers and the public generally. The formulation of policy is the responsibility of the board of directors. Policy incorporates a wide spectrum of operations such as employee relations (which are undergoing considerable revolutionary processes at the present time), policy relating to products and markets, finance and personnel, etc.

Comparative statement. A technique used in budgetary control which enables budgeted and actual performance to be compared and the differences (variances) recorded for managerial attention. The details of budgeted and actual performance are arranged in columns for columnar analysis. It is also possible to compare the performance of the previous year with the current year to establish trends. The statement in a manufacturing company would typically record details relating to operating labour; operating overheads including scrap, rectification, overtime and shift premiums, make-up allowance and waiting time; consumable supplies including items such as small tools, lubricants, stationery and consumable materials; equipment in respect of spares, maintenance and depreciation.

Comparator. A comparator may be a clerk, an automatic device, an electronic device or a computer program which compares the output signal, denoting the actual state of a system, with the desired state. The difference between the two states is a measure of the variance or error. It is the means of computing differences in a system's behaviour which are communicated to appropriate managers so that corrective action can be taken. The process of comparing different factors applies to many business systems and situations which are summarised below:

System	Factors compared
Standard costing	Actual/standard costs
Budgetary control	Actual/budgeted income and expenditure
Stock control	Actual stock/reorder level
	Actual stock/maximum stock
Credit control	Actual account balance/credit limit
Production control	Actual/planned production

Comptroller. *See* CONTROLLER.

Computer aided design (CAD). The use of a computer with sophisticated software for developing designs of various types using a light pen in conjunction with a video screen. The facilities make it possible to modify the shape of an entity and to rotate it for a three-dimensional perspective to assess its features from various angles. The technique enables standard shapes to be stored on disc and accessed when required for incorporation in other designs. It saves considerable time in the design activity and improves quality, as designs can be speedily checked to ensure compatibility with specifications. Errors can be corrected by light pen. The technique is used for a wide range of products and particularly in the design of aircraft, cars and computers.

Conciliation. The procedure of conciliation requires the intervention of a third party in an industrial dispute at the request of either party. The Advisory, Conciliation and Arbitration Service (ACAS) usually arranges this. The conciliator helps the parties to reach an agreement. If this fails the matter may be referred to arbitration (q.v.).

Confederation of British Industry (CBI). Founded in 1965 the CBI was granted a Royal Charter in which its principal objects are laid down. It is concerned with providing British industry with the means of expressing views on industrial, economic, fiscal, commercial, labour, social, legal and technical matters. It also encourages the greater efficiency and competitiveness of British industry. It is an independent body and has no political affiliations. Its membership consists of manufacturing and service-supply companies, trade associations and employers' organisations, including the National Farmers' Union, associations dealing with wholesaling, retailing and distributing, some nationalised industries and the major banking institutions.

Consideration. The price to be paid for goods or services on offer. The price is referred to as the consideration.

Consolidated accounts. The combined accounts of a number of related companies in a group are known as consolidated accounts. They provide details of the overall results of the company as a corporate entity. This applies when the financial accounts of subsidiaries are combined with those of the parent company which is often a holding company (q.v.). The accounts contain a consolidated balance sheet and trading and profit and loss account.

Consultants. *See* MANAGEMENT CONSULTANTS.

Contingency theory. *See* DIRECTING, ORGANISATION THEORY 5 and PIONEERS OF MANAGEMENT.

Contract. A contract is an agreement entered into either by two or more individuals or by directors on behalf of their companies, for a specific purpose, e.g. the construction of a motorway, the building of a power station or a contract of service. A contract can be made by a company's representative in the same form as for an individual, i.e. by deed, in writing or orally. Contracts are enforceable at law.

Contracts of employment. The Contracts of Employment Act 1963 came into force in 1964. It requires employers to provide their workers with a written statement of their terms of employment within 13 weeks of commencing employment with the company. The Act was modified in 1972, one amendment being that the contract of employment need not be written. The contract states the amount of remuneration, period of employment, working hours, holiday entitlements and conditions for giving notice of termination of employment by either party.

Contribution. An accounting term which defines the surplus remaining after deducting the variable cost of sales, known as marginal cost (q.v.), from sales income as indicated below:

Contribution = Sales income − Marginal cost of sales

In marginal costing fixed costs

are not allocated to products but charged against the operating period in which they are incurred. After deducting fixed costs from the contribution a surplus is net profit and a deficiency is a net loss as shown below:

Net profit/loss = Contribution − Fixed costs

Contribution provides the means for assessing the profitability of products because in circumstances when each product appears to be equally profitable this may not be the case when the contribution per unit of limiting factor is taken into account. *See* CONTRIBUTION TO SALES RATIO, CONTRIBUTION PER UNIT OF LIMITING FACTOR and LIMITING FACTOR.

Contribution per unit of limiting factor. In order to maximise profit it is necessary for a business to produce and sell as many units of the product which generates the highest contribution per unit of limiting factor. If there is a shortage of a particular type of labour then production will be curtailed by this resource. If it is assumed that Product A requires 5 hours to manufacture each unit and Product B 6 hours then calculations can be made as follows:

$$\text{Contribution per unit of limiting factor} = \frac{\text{Contribution}}{\text{Limiting factor}}$$

	A	B
Marginal cost	£12.5	£17.5
Selling price	£15.0	£20.0
Contribution	£ 2.5	£ 2.5

On the face of it both products appear to be equally profitable but when the limiting factor is taken into account the situation is somewhat different:

	A	B
Contribution per unit of limiting factor =	£2.5 / 5 hours	£2.5 / 6 hours
	£0.50	£0.42

Product A should be produced in preference to Product B as it requires fewer hours to produce and has a higher contribution per unit of limiting factor.

Contribution to sales ratio. This ratio is extremely important for controlling the profitability of a business as it provides the means of specifying the relative profitability of different products. The ratio is expressed as follows:

$$\text{Contribution to sales ratio} = \frac{\text{Contribution}}{\text{Sales}}$$

Relative profitability may be calculated in the following way:
Assume the selling price and contribution of products A and B are as shown below:

	A	B
	£	£
Selling price per unit	20	10
Variable cost per unit	15	5
Contribution per unit	5	5
Contribution to sales ratio	25% or 25p per £ of sales	50% or 50p per £ of sales

Although the selling prices and variable costs are different, the contribution per unit is identical. This could lead to erroneous conclusions because the contribution to sales ratio of product B is twice that of A. B, therefore, is the product on which to concentrate selling effort in order to maximise profits.

Control. 1. The monitoring process for ensuring that scarce resources are utilised in the most effective and productive way. 2. The term may also be defined as the managerial activity for ensuring the achievement of objectives. An essential requirement for control is information relating to the status of the entity subjected to control. Information is provided by the process of feedback (q.v.). The control process comprises the following elements:
(*a*) Planning the level of performance or objective required to be

achieved which may be defined in terms of standards, budgets, level of activity and control limits whichever is relevant.

(*b*) Collecting details relating to actual system performance in terms of levels of activity, costs and quality, etc.

(*c*) Comparing actual and planned performance for the computation of the deviations.

(*d*) Taking corrective action to modify the state of the system to achieve objectives. *See* CLOSED-LOOP SYSTEM.

Controllable cost or managed cost. This is defined by the ICMA as "A cost, chargeable to a budget or cost centre, which can be influenced by the actions of the person in whom control of the centre is vested".

Controller. The term is generally used to define a senior executive responsible for controlling the financial aspects of an organisation. One organisation may define an official with these responsibilities as a chief accountant, others as administrator, financial director or comptroller. The term is also used in conjunction with specific functional responsibilities but the element of control is still very prevalent. Functional titles using the term controller include production controller, stock controller, quality controller, cost controller, budget controller and credit controller.

Controlling interest. A majority holding of voting shares. More than 50 per cent constitutes a controlling interest.

Control system. *See* CLOSED-LOOP SYSTEM.

Convergence. *See* INFORMATION TECHNOLOGY.

Cooling-off period. An agreed length of time during which normal working practices continue in an industrial dispute to enable negotiations to take place. The period before industrial action is taken.

Co-ordination. As most businesses are organised on a functional basis, it is essential that they operate harmoniously to achieve corporate objectives rather than pursue disjointed uncoordinated objectives. Uncoordinated objectives optimise the performance of specific functions but conflict with the requirements of related functions. As a result, sub-optimisation of the business as a whole occurs. This can be explained by the differing objectives of the sales and production functions: they tend to pursue different goals or at least they would do so if given a free hand. The sales function would generally like to obtain orders regardless of quantity on the basis that an order in the hand is worth two in the hands of a competitor. This philosophy clashes with that of the production function which prefers to operate on the basis of long runs free from disruption, such as the setting up of machines for small orders. Production prefers economic batch sizes which reduce unit costs. Other related functions, e.g. purchasing, personnel, research and development and accounting, must be coordinated within the framework of objectives. The chief coordinator of an industrial company is the managing director, who coordinates the activities of all functions through their respective functional managers utilising the formal chain of command. It is important to appreciate that coordination must be strived for—it does not happen of its own accord. All levels of management have responsibility for coordinating the various activities under their control. Team effort is the keynote of success. *See* OPTIMISATION.

Corporate. 1. A limited company is a

corporate entity having a separate legal identity to its owners, i.e. the shareholders, and the managers of the business, i.e. the directors. Accordingly it can be sued by persons and businesses and can in turn sue persons and businesses. 2. Corporate may also be used to mean the business as a complete entity or a total system. *See also* LIMITED LIABILITY.

Corporate appraisal. This term relates to the activity which appraises corporate strengths and weaknesses on the basis that the ultimate strength of a business can only be as strong as its weakest link. The formal approach to conducting an "internal appraisal" is to assess business strengths and weaknesses for each of the various resources which represent a company's ability to respond to threats and opportunities. This type of appraisal should also embrace managerial and technical competence, as well as the market standing of products and services in relation to those of competitors. The result of conducting this type of evaluation culminates in the preparation of what is known as a capability profile (q.v.). *See* MANAGEMENT DEVELOPMENT.

Corporate capability. *See* CAPABILITY PROFILE.

Corporate objectives. *See* OBJECTIVES.

Corporate planning. *See* STRATEGIC PLANNING.

Corporate policy. *See* COMPANY POLICY.

Corporate strategy. Corporate strategy is the stance to be adopted, as determined by the board of directors, to attain corporate objectives in the long, medium and short term. The determination of a suitable strategy is dependent upon a number of factors including specific strengths and weaknesses inherent in the business, the extent of competition, opportunities and threats. It is also necessary when determining strategy to assess any possible constraints to any proposed course of action. These may relate to shortages of essential raw materials, insufficient plant capacity, cash shortages or falling demand, etc. It is also essential to evaluate the degree of risk in any proposed venture. Deliberations on strategy must first of all consider the following points:

> What is the fundamental economic purpose of the business?
> What type of business should it be?
> What products and services should be marketed?
> What markets should be considered?
> What share of the market is required?
> What rate of growth is required in sales, profits, return on shareholders' investment and share values?
> What lines of credit should be used?

Strategies may be classified as indicated below:

product-market strategy	diversification strategy
divestment strategy	integration strategy
distribution strategy	technological strategy
financial strategy	managerial strategy
research and development strategy	product design strategy
cost reduction strategy	

Refer to specific strategies in this dictionary for further comment.

Cost accounting. This activity may be defined as the application of accounting and costing principles, methods and techniques in the ascertainment of costs and the analysis of variances in order to form a basis for control, assessing profitability and efficiency. Cost accountancy embraces various methods and techniques to suit the needs of different types of business and manufacturing processes.

Methods include job, batch, contract, operation and process costing. Techniques include standard costing (q.v.) and uniform costing (q.v.). *See also* JOB COSTING.

Cost audit. An auditing activity for the purpose of ensuring that costing procedures, methods and techniques are formulated on a sound basis in accordance with established cost accounting principles and practice.

Cost-benefit appraisal. When considering the purchase of a machine such as a jig borer, word processor or mainframe computer, it is essential that all costs, both capital and revenue, are taken into account and related to the expected benefits to assess the economic viability of the project. If the benefits can be expressed in financial terms, such as cost savings, then they can be related to the capital costs incurred to assess the return on the investment. This may be computed as follows:

$$\frac{\text{Savings in cost}}{\text{Capital cost of investment}} \times 100$$

Not all benefits can be expressed in tangible terms, however. Even so such benefits may be very important as they may relate to increased efficiency of accounting routines; improved customer relations, perhaps due to a more speedy and accurate response to enquiries through the use of on-line computer facilities; and improved job satisfaction as a result of personnel using computer terminals instead of ball-point pens during the execution of their duties.

Cost centre. The ICMA define this term as "location, function or items of equipment in respect of which costs may be ascertained and related to cost units for control purposes".

Cost control. The control of all the costs of an undertaking, both direct and indirect, in order to achieve cost effectiveness in business operations. This requires comparison of actual costs to estimates, particularly the direct costs of jobs and contracts, to ensure that estimating is accurately performed and that tasks are performed efficiently. Direct costs are controlled in a mass production environment by the technique of standard costing (q.v.) which compares actual costs with standard costs for the computation of variances to form a basis of control on the exception principle. The technique of budgetary control is applied to the control of the indirect costs of a business, i.e. the overheads. It is necessary to distinguish between fixed and variable costs because the former do not vary with small fluctuations in activity, but variable costs vary directly with variations in activity. *See* COST EFFECTIVENESS, FIXED OVERHEADS and VARIABLE COSTS.

Cost effectiveness. Cost effectiveness is the purpose of cost control techniques to ensure that resources are utilised to the best advantage to maximise the profitability of the business. *See* COST CONTROL.

Cost plus. A term used in association with contracts whereby arrangements are negotiated between the vendor and purchaser (contractor/contractee) to pay all the *costs* incurred in the contract, *plus* an addition for profit. This often applies to circumstances when it is not possible to predetermine the cost of manufacture in advance.

Cost push. An economic term which implies that increases in the cost of manufacturing goods will cause the price of the product to increase causing an inflationary situation. An inflationary spiral may occur because additional wage demands to offset increased prices will aggravate the situation further. *See* INFLATION.

Cost reduction. *See* VALUE ANALYSIS.

Cost reduction strategy. The strategy to be adopted to reduce costs is chosen from a number of viable alternatives or the application of a combination of several different methods. One way is to apply stringent cost control procedures to maintain the standard cost of products and budgeted levels of expenditure as far as possible. Another way is to review all products with a view to reducing their cost by simplifying their design and manufacture or the substitution of less expensive materials provided that the quality or safety of the product is not impaired. *See* VALUE ANALYSIS and COST CONTROL.

Cost standard. *See* STANDARD COST.

Cost variance. The difference between an estimated, or standard cost (q.v.), for an operation or activity and the actual cost incurred. The variances provide the basis for exception reporting (q.v.) as a means of applying management by exception. *See* COST CONTROL.

CPM/cost. *See* CRITICAL PATH ANALYSIS.

Credit control. Many businesses sell to customers on credit, i.e. a credit period of a specified number of days after the date of the invoice, and a credit limit, an amount which should not be exceeded under normal circumstances. These two factors form the basis of credit control. The purpose of the activity is primarily to ensure that all goods are paid for. It is one thing to sell goods and services; it is another to obtain payment. Customers are known as debtors and the amounts they owe form part of the working capital of the business. The amount outstanding in debtors should be converted to cash as soon as possible in order to finance business operations from internal sources. This is much cheaper than bank overdrafts or bank loans. It is also necessary to pay creditors from the funds generated by customers. If debtors are outstanding too long, it may be necessary to obtain external finance which incurs high interest charges.

Critical path analysis. A technique for planning and controlling complex projects consisting of many interrelated activities and events, some of which are performed simultaneously in parallel, and others which are performed sequentially one after the other. The activities are shown diagrammatically forming what is known as a network, which is then analysed to determine the critical path. The critical path is that path through the network which will increase project duration time if any of the activities are delayed. The technique is used for planning the installation of large computer systems, construction of buildings, bridges, ships, sections of motorway and aircraft. Critical path analysis (CPA) also includes the techniques of programme evaluation and review technique (PERT) and critical path method (CPM). There is no fundamental difference between the two techniques except that PERT recognises that the time to complete an activity cannot be predicted with certainty whereas CPM assumes that the time required to complete an activity can be computed precisely. Variations of PERT and CPM include PERT/cost and CPM/cost. These techniques incorporate cost factors so that actual and estimated costs can be compared at each stage of the project for reappraisal and decision making purposes. *See also* NETWORK ANALYSIS.

Critical path method (CPM). *See* CRITICAL PATH ANALYSIS.

Current assets. The assets of a business of a transitory nature which are intended for resale or conversion into a different form during the course of business operations. Initially, raw materials are purchased and the amount unused at the end of the trading period forms part of the current assets as stock on hand. Materials in process at the end of the trading period and the labour incurred in processing them also form part of current assets. Similarly, finished products which remain unsold and products sold to customers which are unpaid for are also current assets. Any cash in hand or at the bank at the end of the period are also classed as current assets, all of which appear on the balance sheet. *See* ASSET.

Current liabilities. Amounts owing by the business which are currently due for payment are referred to as current liabilities. They consist of amounts owing to creditors, bank loans due for repayment, proposed dividends, corporation tax due for payment and expenses accrued due.

Current ratio. This ratio assists in analysing the current financial position of a business. It is computed by relating the total current assets to the total current liabilities as follows:

$$\text{Current ratio} = \frac{\text{Total current assets}}{\text{Total current liabilities}}$$

The ratio should be at least 1.5:1 signifying that the current assets are at least one and a half times as great as the current liabilities. It is also necessary to assess whether the current assets are sufficiently liquid to discharge the current liabilities.

Cybernetics. Cybernetics may be defined as the science of communication and control in man and machine systems. The science revolves around artificial intelligence by providing computers with memories and computational facilities, and information systems which are concerned with sensing events in the environment and responding to them in a suitable manner from inbuilt comparators (q.v.) and effectors. This is the foundation of robotics as found in the Doctor Who series and, indeed, in modern factories for internal movement of raw and processed materials and manufacturing operations performed by automated equipment. The cybernetic control process is identical to that of exception reporting (q.v.) which is the basis of management by exception (q.v.). *See* CLOSED-LOOP SYSTEM.

D

Data. The term is used to describe the details which identify and describe business transactions and which are input to the data processing system for the purpose of producing useful information. Examples of business data include hours worked on jobs by employees as a basis for job costing or variance analysis; number of units ordered by customers for order processing and batch production scheduling; number of units issued to production for assembly purposes; number of holiday bookings received and so on.

Database. 1. A centrally located information file serving the needs of a major function or several related functions. 2. A more ambitious definition defines a database as a collection of structured data supporting the operations of the whole or major areas of a business. It is the focal point of a management information system and is usually supported by a computer. The centralisation of information in a database avoids redundancy, i.e. duplicated data in several related files which is the case with separately structured functional files. As an example a personnel file contains details of employees which are also recorded in the payroll file in respect of such elements as name and address, department, bank, National Insurance number and so on. A database should have facilities for the speedy retrieval of data on demand and for maintaining the data up-to-date. The functioning of a database is facilitated by software in the form of a Database Management System (DBMS). It is important to appreciate that it is data which are stored in a database (sometimes referred to as an information file) but when combinations of related data are retrieved it becomes information. Basic data may be grouped in different combinations for different reporting requirements.

Data processing. An activity performed by the administrative organisation of a business which is concerned with the systematic recording, arranging, filing, processing, retrieving and disseminating of information relating to business operations. The activities provide a valuable supporting role in spheres of business management including control, problem solving and decision making.

De Bono, Edward. *See* LATERAL THINKING.

Debtor control ratio. A ratio for controlling the amount owed by debtors. Used for the purpose of monitoring the number of days' or weeks' sales represented by the amount owed by debtors which may be computed as follows:

$$\frac{\text{Debtors} \times 52}{\text{Annual sales}}$$

The ratio should be calculated on the amount of debtors outstanding at the end of each month and by using a moving annual total (MAT) of sales (by deducting the sales of the corresponding month of the previous year and adding the sales of the corresponding month of the current year). This allows the trend of sales to be included in the calculation rather than an outdated historical amount of the previous year.

Debtors. *See* CREDIT CONTROL.

Decentralisation. A technique for the deployment of resources which may be applied to a number of different situations.

(*a*) As a policy of providing authority and responsibility for decision making and control at the local operating level, e.g. branch works instead of at head office.

(*b*) The deployment of computing facilities to decentralised units to enable data processing to be performed under local control instead of at a centralised computing centre. This should speed up the processing of data and provide reports, documents and schedules earlier.

(*c*) The decentralisation of management services such as work study, organisation and methods and operational research as opposed to a centralised service at group headquarters.

Whether to centralise or decentralise is a matter for local conjecture according to prevailing circumstances. *See* CENTRALISATION.

Decision making. The primary task of managers is to make the right decisions at the right time in order to effect change for the purpose of optimising business performance. As a general rule decisions should be made at the lowest possible level in an organisation, as this allows senior managers more time for making decisions of a more complex nature. The type of decision each manager has authority to make should be clearly defined to avoid ambiguity. Decisions are often made on the basis of control information provided in reports as a result of feedback (q.v.). Decision making and problem solving are correlated as it is necessary to solve problems before it is possible to implement the relevant decision. *See* AUTOMATED DECISIONS and DECISION THEORY.

Decision table. A technique applied to analysing business problems which necessitates the conditions specific to the problem and the actions to be taken when the various conditions arise to be defined. A computer program written for a specific application must provide for branching to appropriate parts of the program when specified conditions are detected in the data after testing for their existence. A decision table enables the branching requirements to be defined precisely without omission or ambiguity. The preparation of complicated program flowcharts is facilitated by a decision table which ensures that all conditions and actions are fully provided for. Deciding which action to take is a decision requirement which is programmed to be dealt with automatically as it accords with standardised rules. *See* AUTOMATED DECISIONS.

Decision theory. Decision theory utilises the scientific approach for choosing alternative courses of action on the basis of mathematical techniques, statistical probabilities and other related techniques to assist the analysis of risk involved with decisions. The courses of action which are possible are referred to as "strategies". These depend upon "states of nature" which produce various "outcomes" which are recorded in a pay-off table. An important concept in decision theory is "expectation" which is the average result or outcome if a particular situation recurs frequently. Expectation can be computed by listing all possible exclusive events, valuing each event, computing (probability of events × value of event) and adding the products. Bayes' rule states that when deciding between two or more alternatives the one with the highest expectation should be selected. *See* BAYES' RULE, EXPECTATION, MAXIMAX RULE, MINIMAX RULE and MAXIMUM LIKELIHOOD RULE.

Decision tree. This is a probability tree incorporating branches leading to alternatives, i.e. decision branches. The alternative branches lead to events that depend on probabilities, i.e. probability branches.

Delegation. The managing director, when informing functional managers what is expected of them in the forthcoming operating period(s), is delegating responsibility and the appropriate degree of authority for achieving specified tasks and objectives. The same considerations recur down the chain of command (q.v.) as the functional managers in turn delegate specific duties to the departmental managers for which they are held accountable. This course of action is known as delegation and is essential, particularly in the larger business, as it is impossible for a single manager to maintain direct control over all his subordinates. When a business grows it is necessary to restructure duties and working relationships by the process of delegation which effectively reduces the number of personnel reporting directly to a superior. This leaves more time at his disposal for planning, coordinating and controlling all the activities for which he is ultimately responsible. *See* "BUCK STOPS HERE, THE" and "PASSING THE BUCK".

Demand forecasting. Sales to customers fluctuate for many different reasons and it is necessary to forecast future demand as a foundation on which to plan future business activity, e.g. production schedules, stock levels, purchases of raw materials, manpower requirements and distribution facilities, etc. A number of forecasting techniques are used, including moving average, which requires the calculation of average demand for a number of past periods as a basis for estimating future demand. Exponential smoothing provides for the difference between a forecast and actual demand as a basis for forecasting the demand for the following period having allowed for what is known as a forecasting error. This is the application of statistical methods to forecasting on the basis of previous results. They take no account of changes in taste, fashion, political and legal influences, inflation and weather conditions and so on. These factors must of necessity be considered in an attempt to foresee future business prospects. Statistics only provide trends which may not apply to future circumstances. *See* EXPONENTIAL SMOOTHING.

Demand pull. An economic term which implies that if there is excessive demand for scarce resources then this will cause the price of the resources to increase causing an inflationary situation. *See* INFLATION.

Democratic management style. A style of management which allows subordinates leeway of thought and action and the encouragement of initiative. It also implements the practice of delegation. This style also accepts the theories of motivation, promoting job interest and encouraging people to set their own goals and determining ways of achieving them. Action is taken when necessary on the philosophy of management by exception. It must be appreciated that the most democratic managers must adopt an autocratic stance once in a while when the need arises. *See*

MANAGEMENT STYLE.

Deterministic system. This type of system enables its output to be predicted without error from a specified input of resources. Business and economic systems do not come into this category, however, as they are highly unpredictable. Deterministic systems are mechanistic as they are designed to operate within the structure of standardised rules, regulations, standard computer programs or mechanical structures depending upon the nature of the system whether it is a business organisation (rules and regulations); a business system run on a computer such as stock control (standardised computer program); a machine tool designed to perform specific tasks according to the mechanical controls manipulated (mechanical structure). *See* PROBABILISTIC SYSTEM.

Development of strategy. The formal development of corporate strategy (q.v.) ensures that important aspects are not overlooked. The stages outlined below serve to illustrate that the development of strategy needs careful consideration to avoid ultimate penalties derived from the selection of inadequate strategies. The stages are:

- identify potential opportunities;
- establish resources required for the potential opportunities;
- evaluate costs and benefits of the several opportunities;
- identify potential risks, threats and uncertainty;
- prepare a league table of costs and benefits of the various opportunities;
- select opportunities on the basis of the Pareto rule, i.e. the 80/20 rule as it is likely that 80 per cent of prospective benefits will be derived from 20 per cent of the opportunities;
- implement plans on the basis of selected strategy;
- monitor performance to assess effectiveness of chosen strategy.

Directing. This element of management is concerned with leadership which many believe is the major determinant of productivity and organisational success. Numerous definitions of leadership have been proposed. It is generally agreed, however, that leadership is the process of directing others to achieve personal or organisational goals. To some leadership has an inspirational connotation wherein the leader inspires the followers to strive for successively greater heights; others see the role of the leader as a more supportive one where the leader assists the followers. In practice, leadership is partly each of these.

There has been extensive research on this topic which has resulted in two major types of theories: 1. *Universalist* theories are those arguing that there is one type of leadership style inherently superior to all others, irrespective of the situation in which it operates. These theories are based largely on observation of leader traits and have resulted in prescriptive statements about what characteristics leaders should possess or how they should behave to be effective. 2. *Contingency* theories, on the other hand, assume that different situations require different styles.

Director. The definition of "management" indicates that directors collectively form a board of directors in a public limited company for managing the business's affairs. The board as a whole makes decisions, which is the reason for convening board meetings to enable policy matters to be discussed and a vote taken on relevant issues—let the majority prevail. Directors may be executive or non-executive. Non-executive directors do not play an active part in the management of the business but executive directors have specific responsibilities delegated to them for controlling a major function such as personnel, finance, production, technical and marketing—all carrying the title director after the function, i.e. financial director, etc. The day-to-day operations are coordinated by the managing director. Directors have a duty to act in good faith for the benefit of the shareholders and not obtain any personal gain from their special position. Directors are expected to be competent and act with a degree of skill that can be reasonably expected from a person of such standing and experience. The term director is also used to describe the senior executive of other types of institution such as the Director of a Polytechnic.

Directors, Institute of. The aims of the Institute are to provide a means of representing the interests of its members, to encourage and assist members to improve their professional competence as business leaders. Members are consulted on policy matters through branch groups which provide headquarters with the views of members for inclusion in policy statements to the government. The membership consists of Fellows, Honorary Fellows, Ordinary Members who must be directors of corporate bodies, and Associate Members who need not be directors.

Discounted cash flow. A technique of computing the present values of future incomes or cost savings obtained from an investment over a specified number of years. The purpose is to determine the most profitable investment from several possible alternatives, each of which may have a different capital outflow and different earning levels or cost savings in specific time periods. The concept implies that future cash flows, income or cost savings, are not worth so much as present cash flows. The reason for this is that money presently available can be invested and earn interest. An investment in one machine may have greater overall cost savings than an alternative machine, but the cost savings from the alternative machine may be obtained earlier and thereby have a greater present value. Present value factors are obtained from preprinted tables but may be computed. Net present value may be computed in the following way:

Assume a machine generates cost savings at the end of each of three years: 1st year, £10,000, 2nd year, £3,000, 3rd year, £2,000 and the cost of the machine was £10,000. Rate of interest is 10 per cent.

Year	Cost savings £	Present value factor	Present value £
1	10,000	0.9091	9,091
2	3,000	0.8264	2,479
3	2,000	0.7513	1,503
Total present value of cost savings			13,073
Less capital cost of investment			10,000
Net present value of investment			3,073

Similar computations are performed for alternative investments and the one with the greater net present value should be selected, all other things being equal.

Discrimination. The laws relating to discrimination in employment are largely intended to prevent employers victimising employees or potential employees on the grounds of sex, marital status, race or their trade union membership and activities. Under the provisions of the following acts legal redress is available to those who claim and can demonstrate that they have been discriminated against by their employer: Equal Pay Act 1970; Sex Discrimination Act 1975; Race Relations Act 1976; Employment Protection (Consolidation) Act 1978. The Equal Opportunities Commission (EOC) and the Commission for Racial Equality (CRE) have been set up to investigate complaints, other than those concerning trade union membership and activities, under these acts and to monitor their effects.

Distribution strategy. This term is used in the context of sales outlets used rather than the means of transport employed. In many instances, the nature of the product determines the most suitable strategy. As an example, the only way of getting early large mainframe computers to the user was directly from the manufacturer. With the advent of the silicon chip, however, small personal and business computers are now available and obtainable from a fast-growing dealer network. The smaller Sinclair-type computer can be obtained through direct mail from the manufacturers, or from a High Street retail outlet such as W.H. Smiths. *See also* CORPORATE STRATEGY.

Diversification strategy. A strategy which enlarges the product range by introducing new products, or extending the range of existing products. This may be achieved by employing specialised equipment or by using existing facilities. The strategy is concerned with achieving a greater market from a greater range of products, in order to maximise profits. The strategy of "not putting all of one's eggs in the same basket". *See also* CORPORATE STRATEGY.

Divestment strategy. To strip or get rid of, which in the context of business strategy relates to the elimination of unprofitable products to achieve rationalisation of the product range. The strategy reflects the benefits of standardisation and variety reduction. The selection of products for divestment can be on the basis of relative contribution. The products with the lowest contribution would generally be eliminated. It would be necessary to assess whether any of the potential products destined for elimination are loss leaders because, if they are, their demise may have an effect on profits. The axe must not be wielded indiscriminately, because whichever products are selected it must be appreciated that the total contribution will be less as a result—unless negative contributions are generated by some of the products. It will be necessary to ensure that the remaining products will compensate for this deficiency, perhaps by additional sales. If the potential strategy is to expand sales and markets for the remainder of the range, then total contribution should be higher. *See also* CORPORATE STRATEGY.

Dividend. A distribution of profits to shareholders on the basis of the number of shares held and the rate of dividend declared. Holders of ordinary shares have a dividend only when there are adequate profits, but are entitled to the whole of the surplus profits after preference shareholders' dividends have been paid. Preference shareholders have a right to a fixed rate of dividend which has preference over any dividend paid to ordinary shareholders.

Dividend cover. A ratio which indicates the number of times the dividends payable are covered by the earnings available to ordinary shareholders. It is an indication of financial prudence as a business should be self-financing by the provision of revenue reserves from earnings. It is, therefore, customary to retain a proportion of the current earnings and not to distribute the full amount as dividends to shareholders. The ratio may be computed as follows:

$$\text{Dividend cover} = \frac{\text{Earnings available to ordinary shareholders}}{\text{Dividend payable}}$$

If it may be assumed that the net profit is £100,000 with no prior charges for preference dividends and the proposed dividend is £28,000 then the computation is as shown below:

$$\text{Dividend cover} = \frac{£100,000}{£28,000} = 3.6 \text{ times approx.}$$

Dividend yield. A ratio which indicates the true yield of shares after allowing for the market value or purchase price of such shares, which may vary greatly from the nominal value. Dividend yield is computed as follows:

$$\text{Dividend yield} = \frac{\text{Nominal value of shares}}{\text{Market value of shares}} \times \text{Rate of dividend}$$

If it is assumed that the market value of shares is £3 and 300,000 ordinary shares have a nominal value of £1 each, then the market value of the shares is £900,000. The rate of dividend, the proposed dividend expressed as a percentage of the nominal value of the ordinary shares, is say

$$\frac{£30,000}{£300,000} \times 100 = 10\%$$

The dividend yield is

$$\frac{£300,000}{£900,000} \times 10\% = 3\tfrac{1}{3}\%$$

E

Earnings yield. A ratio which indicates the earnings (profit) available to ordinary shareholders as a percentage of the ordinary share capital related to the ratio of the nominal value and market value of a share. This is computed as follows:

Earnings yield =

Profit available to ordinary shareholders as a percentage of ordinary share capital × $\dfrac{\text{Nominal value of a share}}{\text{Market value (purchase price)}}$

If the profit available to ordinary shareholders is £50,000 and the ordinary share capital is £500,000, the nominal value of a share is £1 and the market value is £2, then the earnings yield is computed as follows:

$$\frac{£50,000}{£500,000} \times \frac{£1}{£2} = 10\% \times \frac{£1}{£2} = 5\%$$

Economic indicators. Indicators which outline the state of the economy and include base rate, treasury bill rate, Financial Times stock indices, general index of retail prices, tax and price index, index of average earnings of all employees, index of industrial production, gross domestic product, index numbers of retail sales in Great Britain, unemployment and sterling effective exchange rate.

Economic order quantity (EOQ). A quantity which minimises total costs, i.e. the sum of storage costs and ordering costs. An annual quantity can be purchased on one order and put into storage until needed. In this instance, it is obvious that only one order is being placed for a complete year's requirements, in which case ordering costs are at a minimum but storage costs are at a maximum. If the whole of a year's supply is put into storage it signifies that, on average, half of the items will be in storage for the whole year. By trial and error, computing costs for different ordering frequencies, it is possible to compute that quantity which minimises total cost: this is the quantity to order. Storage costs and ordering costs oppose each other because the greater the quantity in store the higher the storage costs, but the ordering costs are lower and vice versa. The EOQ can be computed by a simple formula as an alternative to trial and error methods. The formula is as follows:

$$EOQ = \sqrt{\frac{2PY}{IU}}$$

where:
P = Cost of placing an order (ordering costs)
Y = Annual rate of demand (quantity)
I = Stock holding cost as a decimal value of average stock value (storage costs)
U = Unit cost

Economics. A subject which deals with the study of costs, prices, demand, supply, location of industry, distribution, production, levels of employment (or unemployment) by region, markets, monopoly industries, and profits, etc. Economics deals with all aspects of business, industries and the national economic system as a whole and how it interacts with the international economic system. International economics deals largely with trade and financial transactions between countries.

Economic studies are often divided into microeconomics and macroeconomics. Microeconomics is concerned with the economics of small units, i.e. studies of firms, industries and industrial and governmental relationships. Macroeconomics deals with overall matters, such as fiscal policy, inflation, monetary policy, employment and consumption.

Effector. 1. In a managerial context, effectors consist of line managers responsible for production, marketing and other functions. They are responsible for implementing or modifying plans (the process of "effecting") and ensuring they are acted upon and that corrective action is taken when necessary. In other words, an effector is a manager who effects change to modify the state of a system, i.e. the use of resources and levels of performance in order to achieve objectives. 2. In a cybernetic context, an effector adjusts the controlled variable by modifying the input of resources (men, money, materials, machines) to adjust the status of the system performance in accordance with the magnitude of the error signal (variance), in order to achieve the reference input (objective) and attain a state of homeostasis (stable state). 3. In automated systems an effector may be an electronic device which automatically adjusts the action of the system. A thermostat, for instance, automatically switches the heater on or off according to the temperature of the water required in a central heating system.

Electronic computer. A computer may be defined as a machine which accepts data from an input device, performs arithmetical and logical operations in accordance with a predefined program, and finally transfers the processed data to an output device either for further processing or in final printed form. A computer consists of a series of related machines, i.e. input, storage and output devices and a processor. The term "electronic brain" is sometimes used to describe an electronic computer because of its phenomenal power in performing calculations and other related operations. A computer, however, is not capable of original thought in the way humans are. A computer cannot out-think but it can out-perform humans. They are used throughout industry and commerce for many and varied tasks, from preparing a payroll and booking a holiday, to controlling the actions of an automated production line.

Electronic data processing. The processing of business data to produce meaningful information by means of electronic data processing equipment which is usually some type of electronic computer, either a micro, mini or mainframe, either on a stand-alone basis or as part of a network. *See* DATA PROCESSING.

Elements of management. The constituent elements which provide the foundations of management. The elements are relevant to all types of business whether an airline, insurance company, building society or manufacturing business. They also relate to all levels of management to a greater or lesser degree. Some elements predominate in various organisations and within the various functions of an organisation. Opinions may differ regarding the factors which constitute the elements of management, but typically they are planning, organising, staffing, directing, controlling, coordinating, problem solving and decision making. See specific headings for further definitions.

Employers' associations. A joint body of employers primarily formed for the purpose of conducting negotiations with trade unions.

Employment agencies. Agencies which assist in placing suitable candidates to vacant positions. An agency may provide an expeditious way of locating staff as they may have suitable candidates on record. This avoids unnecessary advertising expenditure and delay. If suitable candidates are not available, an agency will advertise on behalf of clients. Agencies charge for their services on the basis of a percentage of starting salary plus advertising expenses. The client only pays for successful appointments.

Equal opportunities. *See* DISCRIMINATION.

Equity capital (equity shares). The issued share capital of a company which carries the right to the whole of the profits remaining after payment of dividends to preference shareholders (q.v.). *See* CAPITAL.

Equity theory. *See* MOTIVATION THEORY 4.

Ergonomics. The science which ensures that working environments, operations and equipment are suitable for the needs of workers and consumers. The science attempts to locate dials and controls within easy vision and reach of workers and operators (car drivers for instance) to avoid excessive eye and physical strain. As a result, operations are performed in relative comfort and, in the case of manufacturing activities, at a high level of productivity. The design of products, such as office furniture and motor cars, is carefully considered to take account of the most comfortable posture for performing specific tasks. Car seats are styled to be comfortable and to be at the correct height for observing warning lights and manipulating controls. The British Standards Institution define ergonomics as "The relation between man and his occupation, equipment and environment and, particularly, the application of anatomical, physiological and psychological knowledge to the problems arising therefrom."

Exception reporting. The process of providing information for management control which is restricted to that which discloses significant variances to planned performance whether in the use of materials, machines, manpower, money or variations in the state of the market. Such reports focus managements' attention to significant situations immediately, allowing them to respond much more quickly than if they had to wade through voluminous details. The technique is an efficient means of feedback, i.e. communicating environmental data to the controlling authority in an adequate timescale to stimulate timely and effective action. Only in this way is it possible to achieve objectives efficiently. *See* FEEDBACK.

Executive. 1. An organisational relationship which exists between superiors and subordinates, i.e. line relationships. These are the formal authority relationships of a business. 2. An alternative term for a senior manager or director, often referred to as an executive as they are responsible for executing business policy and decisions made by the board of directors. All directors are not executives, however. Non-executive directors (q.v.) do not participate in the day-to-day management of the business.

Expectancy theory. *See* MOTIVATION THEORY 5.

Expectation. This is one of the most important concepts in decision theory. "Expectation" is the average result which can be achieved if a particular set of circumstances occurs regularly. It is usual to define "expectation" in monetary terms. *See* MAXIMUM LIKELIHOOD RULE.

Expediting. A term which describes an all-too-familiar business situation concerned with getting things done. Expediting is the activity concerned with encouraging situations to achieve defined events, such as receipt of an order for materials at a stated time and place, or earlier if possible. The term is used in the production environment as an alternative term to "progressing" orders, jobs or parts through the various production operations and processes to achieve the required quantity at the right time. The activity is concerned with avoiding or eliminating problems in the production activities and eliminating delays in shipping goods to customers.

Expenditure. The amount of money expended on a service, materials, overheads or plant and machinery. Expenditure is normally classified in accounting systems according to the nature of the expenditure for control purposes. Expenditure on materials is classified by type, primarily to distinguish between those of a direct and indirect nature again for accounting and control purposes. Expenditure relating to wages is also analysed into direct and indirect categories to facilitate costing and budgetary control.

Exponential smoothing. The technique of forecasting which provides for the correction of previous forecasting errors. Very rarely will a forecast match up with the subsequent actual value, referred to as the actual observation. The difference between the forecast and the actual observation is used as the basis for forecasting the following period. The difference is referred to as the forecasting error. The full extent of the error is not applied, however, since a proportion of the error is due to random variations. A correction factor, known as a smoothing constant, is applied to the error and this varies between 0 and 1. The smoothing constant exponentially smooths averages by giving a different weight (significance) to earlier periods compared to later periods. It is usual to use a smoothing constant of 0.1 or 0.2 and once this has been established it remains unchanged. The degree of sensitivity in forecasting is dependent upon the value of the smoothing constant. *See* DEMAND FORECASTING.

External audit. *See* AUDITOR.

External auditor. *See* AUDITOR.

F

Factor comparison method. A system or method of job evaluation whereby specific factors are analysed and compared, in order to determine the relative worth of each job. The factors which are analysed include responsibility for the control of machines, number of employees responsible for, skill required, mental effort necessary, physical requirements and working conditions.

Factors of production. An economic term used to describe the resources required to facilitate the production of goods including land, labour and capital (q.v.). The efficient production of goods requires the correct mix of resources otherwise shortages of one, e.g. capital, leads to constraints and surpluses of others, e.g. labour, leading to idle facilities. *See also* FACTORY SYSTEM.

Factory. A term used to describe a building or structure in which machines and/or labour are employed for the manufacture of saleable products.

Factory cost. The cost incurred during the manufacture of products, frequently referred to as production cost. It comprises prime cost (q.v.) plus absorbed production overheads (q.v.). Factory cost excludes costs in respect of marketing, research and development and administration.

Factory management. *See* WORKS MANAGEMENT

Factory system. A system whereby workers and machines are assigned to specific parts of a building, i.e. a factory, for the purpose of performing production or manufacturing operations, i.e. the conversion of basic raw materials into saleable products. A factory system brings together the factors of production (q.v.).

Fayol, Henri (1841–1925). *See* ORGANISATION THEORY 2 and PIONEERS OF MANAGEMENT.

Feasibility study. The term is often used in association with investigations to determine the viability of using, or not using, a computer in a business. It is a systematic appraisal of procedures, methods and systems in an office or factory to establish the feasibility of converting the administrative systems to computerisation, or the automation of factory processes, in order to reduce the level of manpower and operating costs, thus providing a more effective and productive organisation. It is also necessary to conduct feasibility studies in many business situations in order to provide sufficient facts of the situation to enable management to make adequate judgment on a proposed course of action. It is necessary, for instance, to conduct market research to determine whether it is feasible to launch a new product in an existing market or enter a new market with an existing product.

Investment appraisal techniques also provide the facts for assessing the feasibility of one investment compared to another after considering the inherent risk factors.

Feedback. The communication of a system's measured output to a comparator (q.v.) for the detection of deviations from the required performance. Refer to **Closed-loop system**. It is important to appreciate, however, that in cybernetics (q.v.) two forms of feedback are considered, i.e. negative and positive. Most business control systems are "negative" error actuated systems. The actual behaviour of the system is compared with the desired behaviour and the differences are detected as positive deviations (errors); action is effected in the opposite direction to counteract them. On the other hand, the characteristics of some types of systems are such that the detected deviations need to be amplified. Amplification applied to servo-mechanisms whereby a small manual force is detected and amplified to achieve a defined purpose. For example, a small manual force applied to aircraft controls is detected and amplified to the force necessary to adjust the control surfaces, which would be beyond the normal strength of the pilot. If unfavourable deviations in business systems are amplified, then errors would be amplified causing the system to deteriorate even further. There may be instances, however, when the amplification of deviations may be of benefit. This could apply when a lower priced material to standard is used in production which proves to be adequate for the purpose. This situation should be exploited, i.e. amplified. There are cases when a delay in applying the result of feedback generates the opposite effect to that required, i.e. positive feedback instead of negative. For instance, if an unfavourable production output is detected and action is taken too late to alter the situation, then it is out of phase because the state of the system has changed in the meantime. Action is taken to remedy a situation which no longer exists. This is known as the "delay factor". In this instance the output may have already increased and the effect of the negative feedback is to amplify the increase in output even further, rather than merely offset the previous shortfall.

Feedforward. The error signals generated by a system are usually used to adjust the current input to a system to optimise its performance (feedback). However error signals monitored over a period may also be used as a basis for planning the future use of resources (feedforward). This technique ensures that the historical trend, or inherent behaviour, of a system is allowed for when setting control parameters for future activities.

Finance. Matters relating to the supply and demand of monetary resources in a business during the normal course of business activities. Also relates to activities concerned with raising capital, payment of dividends, arranging loans and overdrafts.

Finance Act. An Act which outlines the government's fiscal proposals for the current year. Each year the Chancellor of the Exchequer presents budget proposals which form the foundation of a subsequent Finance Bill. The Bill becomes a Finance Act after being subjected to Parliamentary debates and amendments.

Finance company. An organisation which provides credit and hire purchase agreements to individuals and businesses. Many finance companies are subsidiaries of banks. They obtain security for loans or hire purchase agreements by way of the assets purchased with the finance advanced.

Financial accountant. A financial accountant is responsible for planning and controlling all accounting procedures of a financial nature, monitoring accounting systems, supervising the preparation and distribution of periodic and annual accounting statements, reports and statistics including profit and loss accounts and balance sheets; ensuring that all business transactions are recorded in proper books of account;

controlling the receipt and payment of cheques; ensuring that statutory records are maintained in respect of wages and salaries; safeguarding the assets of the business in respect of plant and machinery, stocks, debtors and cash; implementing internal check procedures; maintaining a record of assets and depreciation in the plant register, etc.

Financial management. Embraces the management of all financial and costing aspects of business operations, including planning and controlling revenue and capital expenditure, implementing the financial policy of the board, informing the board of significant matters relating to cash flows, profits, losses and expenditure variances to the budget and preparation of periodic reports for the board. Arranging short term finance, i.e. bank loans and overdrafts, planning further share issues, the valuation of shares of other businesses as going concerns as a prerequisite to possible takeover bids or amalgamations. Assessing asset replacement values and ensuring that sufficient reserves are maintained for future replacements and maximising the return on investments. The financial management of a large public company is the responsibility of a financial director, or company secretary, who may indeed be one and the same person.

Financial ratios. Ratios are a useful way of presenting financial information in an easily understandable form and accordingly this type of ratio is of interest to management, shareholders, creditors and bankers. Financial ratios include those relating to dividend cover (q.v.), dividend yield (q.v.), earnings yield (q.v.) and price/earnings ratio (q.v.), etc.

Financial statement. A financial statement is a report which indicates the financial status of a complete business, or part of a business, at a stated moment in time, or for a specified period of time. These statements also provide details of the changes which have occurred from one period to another, shown on comparative balance sheets and profit and loss accounts. They also record the variances between budgeted and actual results. *See* BALANCE SHEET and PROFIT AND LOSS ACCOUNT.

Financial strategy. Financial strategy is concerned with establishing the most suitable ways and means of financing business operations, including matters relating to operating expenses, capital expenditure in respect of buildings and plant replacement, share issues and dividend policy, etc. The strategy to determine the most suitable source for financing an expansion programme is of paramount importance with regard to the period of the loan and interest charges to be incurred. Financial strategy must also consider lines of credit available; lease *v* purchase options in respect of cars, plant and machinery; sale and lease-back deliberations regarding buildings and/or land; capital gearing and matters relating to inflation accounting. *See also* CORPORATE STRATEGY.

Financial year. A financial year normally embraces a twelve month period at the end of which year-end accounts and accounting statements, i.e. balance sheet (q.v.), trading account (q.v.) and profit and loss account (q.v.) are prepared. The financial year can be any consecutive twelve month period but usually commences from the date when the business started. External auditors inspect books of account at the year-end to ensure they present a true and fair view. *See* AUDITOR.

First-line management. This category of management consists of supervisors in charge of working groups. They may be known as chargehands, section or group leaders. They normally report to a senior supervisor known as a foreman. First-line management is responsible for controlling the activities of personnel within the section or group they are working with, often as working supervisors. They implement the instructions of foremen, allocate work to each member of the group, control their performance and inspect the quality of their work.

Fixed assets. This class of asset includes those of a tangible nature having a specific value and which are not consumed during the course of business and trade but provide the means for producing saleable goods or providing services. Fixed assets include the land on which offices and factory buildings are sited in which are located various items of plant and machinery, all of which constitute fixed assets. Land and buildings tend to appreciate in value in an inflationary economy, but plant and machinery depreciate through the effluxion of time and wear and tear. The value of these assets is reduced accordingly. The balance sheet records the original cost of assets, unless revalued in the case of land and buildings to realisable values, and also shows the depreciation, when applicable, and the net book value. *See* CAPITAL RESERVE.

Fixed budget. The ICMA define a fixed budget as "A budget which is designed to remain unchanged irrespective of the volume of output or turnover attained". This is in distinction to a flexible budget (q.v.) which is designed to change with the level of activity attained. The disadvantage of a fixed budget is the inaccuracy of variances, as differences in the level of activity affect the level of variable overheads incurred, whereas fixed overheads (q.v.), as the name implies, do not vary with the level of activity. Inaccuracies are reflected in the following data which serves to provide a basis for comparing the variances obtained when using fixed budgets and when using flexible budgets.

Budgeted output	1,000 units
Budgeted overheads:	
Fixed	£10,000
Variable	£ 5,000 (£5 per unit)
Total	£15,000
Overhead rate per unit	
$\frac{£15,000}{1,000}$ =	£15
Actual output	800 units
Actual expenditure (total overheads)	£14,000

Variance analysis fixed budget basis:

	£
(a) Overheads absorbed 800 units × £15 per unit	12,000
(b) Budgeted overheads (based on 1,000 units)	15,000
(c) Actual overheads incurred	14,000

The difference between (a) and (b) is an adverse volume variance of £3,000, as the overheads absorbed by the actual output is lower than the budgeted overheads. The difference between (b) and (c) is a favourable expenditure of £1,000 as the budgeted overheads are greater than the actual overhead expenditure incurred. The difference between (a) and (c) is an adverse overhead variance of £2,000 which may be stated as being due to an adverse volume variance and an offsetting favourable expenditure variance. These variances do not disclose the correct situation as the overheads include variable overheads in respect of units not produced.

Variance analysis flexible budget basis:
As 200 units have not been produced compared to the number budgeted, it is necessary to flex the variable overheads in accordance with the level of activity achieved, that is 800 units, as follows:

	£
(a) Overheads absorbed 800 units × £15 per unit	12,000
(b) Budget overhead allowance: £	
Fixed overheads 10,000	
Variable overheads (800 units × £5 per unit) 4,000	
	14,000
(c) Actual overheads incurred	14,000

The difference between (a) and (b) is an adverse volume variance of £2,000, not £3,000 as indicated above, due to fixed overheads not being absorbed on 200 units not produced compared to those budgeted. There is no expenditure variance in this case.

Fixed cost. *See* FIXED OVERHEADS.

Fixed overheads. This is a type of overhead which is fixed within specified circumstances and does not fluctuate with the level of activity, unless additional production facilities need to be provided for increased activity. Such costs relate to the provision of facilities, such as land and buildings, plant and machinery and management salaries, which enable business operations to be performed. It is important to appreciate that although fixed overheads do not vary in total with fluctuations in activity, they do vary on a unit basis, i.e. the fixed cost per unit varies inversely to the level of activity. This means that the fixed cost per unit increases as activity decreases and decreases as activity increases.

Assume activity level = 2,000 units
Calculation of overhead cost per unit =
$\frac{\text{Fixed overhead (total)}}{\text{Number of units}} = \frac{£20,000}{2,000} = £10$
Activity level decreases to 1,000 units
Calculation of overhead cost per unit =
$\frac{£20,000}{1,000} = £20$
Activity level increases to 2,500 units
Calculation of overhead cost per unit =
$\frac{£20,000}{2,500} = £8$

Flexible budget. This is defined by the ICMA as "A budget which, by recognising the difference in behaviour between fixed and variable costs in relation to fluctuations in output, turnover, or other variable factors such as number of employees is designed to change appropriately with such fluctuations."
See FIXED BUDGET AND VARIABLE OVERHEADS.

Floating assets. *See* CURRENT ASSETS.

Flow production. A production technique having processes linked, either mechanically as in manufacturing flowlines, or by means of pipes, ducts and pressure vessels in chemical and distillation flow processes. The technique achieves high levels of productivity and high utilisation of resources as it eliminates laborious manual handling operations between processes. It is not necessary to have a mass production environment before applying the technique, but mass production situations need to use the technique to achieve the required level of output. Major breakdowns of equipment can be disruptive as flowlines can be brought to a standstill even though only one part of the line may be affected. The technique requires a steady demand for the product to achieve a high utilisation ratio. It tends to be highly capital intensive and have operating costs of a fixed nature predominate, including such expenses as plant depreciation, rent and rates of floor space, insurance and maintenance costs.

Follett, Mary Parker (1868–1933). *See* LAW OF THE SITUATION.

Forecasting. *See* DEMAND FORECASTING.

Foreman. *See* FIRST-LINE MANAGEMENT.

Formal relationships. May be defined as the operating relationships which exist in a business and which are formally structured in the organisation to achieve the required objectives. They include the formal direct lines of authority for giving commands and for receiving information (feedback, q.v.) on the status of operations from subordinates.

Free enterprise. The process of allowing an economy to function without central control from the government but allowing the laws of supply and demand to act as an automatic regulator. Individuals and businesses as a whole perform economic activities as long as there is sufficient demand for their goods and services. This produces a competitive economy.

Free trade. The process of conducting international trade free from import and export quotas, tariffs and other controls.

Frequency distribution. A statistical table including the number of times (occurrences) an event or entity occurs. The entities may be ungrouped, or grouped into classes, by means of a class interval, e.g. sales 0–500, 501–1000, 1001–1500, etc. Grouping allows the significance of data to be more easily assessed. A frequency distribution enables variances and standard deviations to be computed.

Function. A function may be defined as a major business activity which is controlled by a functional manager (q.v.) with wide experience of the specific function for which he is responsible. Examples of functions in a manufacturing and marketing oriented business include production, marketing, personnel, inspection, production control, accounting, R & D, stock control, purchasing and maintenance, etc.

Functional budget. The ICMA define a functional budget as "A budget of income and/or expenditure applicable to a particular function." Such budgets are required for each business function and provide a basis for controlling the income and level of expenditure as stated in the definition. Separate budgets are required for detailing items to be purchased and produced in specified periods, in addition to the normal functional budgets which primarily detail expenditure on specific items such as manpower, rectification, scrap, waiting time, holiday pay, electricity, small tools, consumable supplies, etc.

Functional managers. A manager responsible for the efficient operation of a business function. His duties embrace those attributable to any manager, i.e. planning, co-ordinating, staffing, organising, motivating, controlling, problem solving and decision making. *See* FUNCTION.

Functional objectives. Objectives relating to specific business functions, i.e. production, sales, purchasing, accounting and personnel, etc. Such objectives must be specified and coordinated with corporate objectives and stated in unambiguous quantitative terms whenever possible so that they can be expressed precisely and be readily understood. Examples are: increase sales of product A by x per cent; increase profitability of product B by y per cent; increase market share of all products by z per cent. These marketing objectives must be reconciled with production objectives which may be stated as: increase production of product A by y per cent; reduce costs of product B by z per cent; increase production of all products by z per cent.

Functional organisation. In practice it is not possible to have such an organisation because the term functional relates to the organisation of work on the basis of specialisation. A purely functional organisation structure implies that each specialist conveys his instructions direct to personnel, rather than through a formal chain of command. It is said that this type of organisation creates too many bosses, i.e. too many specialists giving orders to personnel, which leads to confusion as orders tend to conflict with each other. If the duties of each specialist are well defined, however, conflicting orders should not arise but this type of organisation would not work in most instances. This type of organisation was devised by F.W. Taylor, one of the founders of scientific management. *See* FUNCTION.

Functional relationship. Functional departments provide a service to line managers in respect of work study, maintenance, purchasing of materials, control of stocks, controlling quality and so on. If these activities were not performed by specialist functions, then the line organisation would need to perform them themselves. The relationship between personnel in the various functions is, therefore, of a functional nature rather than a line relationship.

Functional responsibilities. *See* FUNCTION and FUNCTIONAL MANAGERS.

Funds flow analysis. *See* SOURCE AND DISPOSITION OF FUNDS STATEMENT.

G

Gain. In a business context the term infers a surplus of income over expenditure which is referred to either as gross profit (q.v.) or net profit (q.v.).

Gantt chart. *See* BAR CHART.

Gap analysis. *See* STRATEGIC GAP.

Gearing. A term which refers to the relationship between fixed interest capital, i.e. prior charge capital (preference shares, q.v.), and equity share capital (q.v.), i.e. ordinary share capital. When fixed interest capital is a higher proportion than the equity capital the company is said to be high geared. The reverse applies when the fixed interest capital is a lower proportion than equity capital, then it is low geared. When business profits are declining the preference shareholders have first claim on the available profits which means there may be very little left, if any, for the ordinary shareholders. However, when profits are increasing it is the ordinary shareholders who are likely to benefit as they are entitled to the whole of the surplus profits, after the rights of preference shareholders have been satisifed.

General manager. A senior manager having responsibility for a major section of a business with responsibility for controlling several functions or departments in some organisations. A general manager may, in some instances, report to a managing director. It all depends upon the nature, structure and size of the business.

Gilbreth, Frank and Lillian. *See* ORGANISATION THEORY 1 and PIONEERS OF MANAGEMENT.

Goals. May be defined as targets for achievement in pursuit of specific aims and objectives. In order to accomplish long-range objectives, it is necessary to achieve short-term goals which may be classed as stepping stones to aid progress along the desired path. Goals may be defined within budgets which include details of performance levels required in respect of sales, production, costs, manpower and stocks.

Going concern. A business which performs its normal business activities profitably, i.e. obtains an adequate return on its capital. Assets are valued on their profit earning capacity rather than realisable value, which would be the case in respect of a business going into liquidation. Bank managers assess the viability of a business on its profit earning record, when determining whether it is a good or bad risk, before granting loans to finance business expansion or for short-term working capital needs.

Going rate. The rate for the job, i.e. the normal wage rate for the industry or area for a specific class of work or trade.

Golden handshake. Compensation paid to a director or senior executive for premature loss of office. This often occurs as a result of takeovers, or mergers, when the combined management strength is surplus to requirements of the major restructured business.

Good faith. Business or private transactions undertaken honestly without intention to mislead.

Goodwill. An intangible asset which can only have a value, i.e. a realisable value, when a business is sold, if at all. The value of goodwill may be nil if a business is unprofitable or belongs to a declining industry, or has a poor site value. Goodwill has a tangible value when a profitable business is sold, or has a valuable site value, or a good trading reputation. If goodwill has a tangible value it can be computed on the basis of an agreed number of years' super profits, i.e. surplus profits to the level normally earned in a similar type of business in respect of turnover, asset values and costs, etc. If profits fluctuate year to year, then goodwill would perhaps be better computed on the basis of average profits. For example, if the normal annual profits for a specific type of business are £10,000 and the following profits earned by a particular business over the last five years:

	£		£
Year 1	12,000	Year 4	12,000
Year 2	13,000	Year 5	14,000
Year 3	14,000		

It is first necessary to compute the average profits which is £65,000/5 = £13,000. Super profits are the surplus between the normal profits of £10,000 and £13,000, i.e. £3,000. If it is agreed to purchase four years super profits, then the valuation for goodwill is 4 × £3,000 = £12,000. If the company's capital was £100,000 then average profits of £13,000 represent a return on investment of 13%. The normal return expected is 10%, i.e. £10,000 normal profits related to capital of £100,000. There are other methods of calculation, that outlined above is one example of how goodwill may be computed. Goodwill is normally valued at cost for the balance sheet and should never be increased in value, as it is not good practice to provide for unrealised increases in goodwill. In fact, if a company is able to write down goodwill, then this is real evidence of its existence as it creates a reserve; the assets shown on the balance sheet will be those of a tangible nature only.

Go-slow. Workers, when going-slow, perform their duties and tasks at a slower than normal pace, as part of an industrial dispute. The aim is to disrupt the smooth operation of the business in which they are employed.

Governor. 1. The term is used as an alternative to controller (q.v.). 2. The term is sometimes used colloquially to mean "the boss" or the cockney equivalent—"governor". 3. One who controls the activities of others. 4. The technical derivative is as follows. The Watt governor is usually regarded as the first manmade control mechanism whereby the speed of an engine was controlled by a governor with weighted arms, mounted on pivots so that they are free to rise by centrifugal force as they revolve. The arms turn at an increasing speed as the engine speed increases. The arms operate a valve which admits energy to the engine. The arms rise higher as the engine speed increases and the valve is closed proportionately, thereby reducing the amount of energy supplied to the engine thus limiting its speed, i.e. to govern its performance. If the engine fails to attain a given speed the arms are positioned so that the valve is opened more, admitting more energy until the required speed is reached. The required output, the defined engine speed, is achieved by self-regulation as the input to the engine is adjusted by its own output on the feedback principle. Self-regulation such as this is not usually possible for managerial tasks which is why managers are required. The governor was controlling or managing the speed of the engine.

Gross profit. The surplus remaining after deducting from sales income the manufacturing cost of goods sold.

The manufacturing cost is the sum of direct material, wages and expenses and manufacturing overheads, i.e. indirect costs (q.v.). It must be noted that gross profit is computed before deducting administration, financial and selling and distribution overheads.

Gross profit as a percentage of sales. An important ratio for business control as it provides a measure of the gross earnings in relation to sales. Two factors can affect the gross profit percentage, i.e. sales price and manufacturing cost of sales. Variations in either can affect the percentage but it should not fluctuate unduly except in exceptional circumstances, e.g. when increases occur in the cost of raw materials and wage rates in advance of sales price increases. Fixed overheads (q.v.) also fluctuate as a rate per unit for variations in the volume of production.

Group Capacity Assessment (GCA). A work measurement and control technique developed by Arthur Young & Co., which is applied in clerical, accounting, stores, supply and reprographic areas of a business. The GCA programme is designed to equip supervision and management with an effective means of monitoring the performance of their departments and of budgeting future staff requirements. The work measurement techniques are used to establish a department's, or group's, work-load by providing group work standards.

Group dynamics. A technique applied to the study of groups of people to assess the behaviour of individuals and how they interact with, and influence, other members of the group and the group as a whole.

Growth rate. The annual increase in the output or sales of a business, or economy as a whole, expressed as a ratio of the previous year's achievements.

Guesstimate. An approximation which falls mid-way between an inspired guess and a calculated estimate, based on as many factors as the situation allows. Management and administrative staff often have to make guesstimates in the absence of complete information in order "to keep the pot boiling". This is not to say, however, that guesstimates are wild hunches: sometimes they are, but in the main they are carefully considered appraisals.

H

Head hunting. The practice of recruitment agencies who directly approach key personnel of a business in an attempt to induce them to leave their present employment, by the offer of higher salaries and other benefits if they join their client's business.

Health and safety. It goes without saying that the health and safety of the personnel of an organisation are of paramount importance whilst undertaking all types of industrial activities. The legal requirements are contained in the Factories Act 1961 and the Offices, Shops and Railway Premises Act 1963. These Acts stipulate the minimum requirements relating to health and safety of people at work. Matters which come within the sphere of the Acts include heating, lighting, ventilation, toilet facilities, guards for machinery, etc.

The Health and Safety at Work etc. Act 1974 requires employers to take a number of major steps to maintain a satisfactory working environment. The principle requirements are: to explain to personnel concerned the correct way in which plant and equipment should be operated; to ensure that employees understand the responsibilities to themselves and to fellow workers; to provide training as appropriate; to inform employees of health and safety policies and the names of safety officers; to make provision for safety representatives appointed by recognised trade unions. Both employers and employees can be prosecuted under the Act for offences against the interests of health, safety and welfare. The maximum penalties are an unlimited fine and/or two years' imprisonment.

Herzberg, F. See MOTIVATION THEORY 2.

Heterogeneous organisation structure. This form of organisation is designed to fulfil a specific purpose and all the various activities required to accomplish it are grouped together heterogeneously. It is also referred to as a "vertical" organisation structure or "purpose" organisation which may be grouped on the basis of commodities for effective organisation of the purchasing function; by sales area to enable customers' requirements and after-sales service to be accomplished more efficiently; or product manufacturing to facilitate the efficient manufacture of specific products by concentrating all operations and processes on specific products according to requirements.

Hierarchy of Needs. See MOTIVATION THEORY 1.

Heuristics. A trial and error technique of problem solving by interactive methods. The technique is related to simulation. The term heuristics is of Greek origin meaning "discovery". The technique is used when it is not possible to use mathematical formulae as the system in question behaves in a random manner.

Hierarchical objectives. The hierarchical organisation structure (q.v.) as depicted below generates the need for objectives to be established for each level of management, i.e. senior, middle and first line management. Only by this means is it possible to achieve the overall objectives of the business. See FUNCTIONAL OBJECTIVES.

Hierarchical organisation structure. This form of organisation, when plotted on an organisation chart, forms what is known as an organisation pyramid. Different levels of management are automatically created when delegation is implemented in the various functions. This causes a pyramid effect from the apex, consisting of senior managers in charge of functions, to the base, consisting of first line supervisors in charge of sections and groups. In between is the middle management strata with departmental responsibility. The primary concept is that each subordinate can only have one boss (superior) who is situated immediately above him in the pyramid; this is the chain of command throughout the business.

High geared. *See* GEARING.

Histogram. A graphical representation of a frequency distribution (q.v.) consisting of rectangles drawn in relation to a specified scale to represent specific values, such as the number of rejects in specific batches of production. It is a useful means of presenting information, as graphical representation of data has an immediate impact. The facts disclosed are immediately interpreted in a meaningful way.

Historical costing. A method of costing which is effected after production or fabrication is completed, i.e. "post" costing as contrasted with the "precosting" technique of standard costing which is applied when standard products are manufactured. Historical costing is applied in batch, job or contract environments when orders differ according to the specific needs of the customer. Data relating to direct materials, labour and expenses are collected and recorded on prime documents such as material issue notes, job tickets and expense vouchers. The details are recorded on job or contract cost sheets. It is usual to apply a proportion of the fixed overheads of the business to each job or contract by some suitable absorption method so that all work undertaken has a fair share of general overheads. The details shown on the cost sheets are compared with estimates to assess any deviations which may require renegotiation with customers in certain instances. The accuracy of preparing estimates is, therefore, also monitored.

Holding company. A company which owns all the shares, or has a majority shareholding, in several other companies and as a consequence has financial control over their activities. The holding company acquires the shares of the companies it controls in exchange for shares in the new company. Profits are paid as dividends to the holding company which distributes them to its shareholders.

Homeostasis. The process of maintaining the performance of a system on a stable basis despite random influences from the environment. *See* CLOSED LOOP SYSTEM and ADAPTIVE SYSTEM.

Homogeneous organisation structure. This form of organisation is designed for performing specific activities or processes on the principle of specialisation. All machines and personnel concerned with a specific type of work or process are grouped together to achieve maximum productivity. This type of organisation facilitates supervision because of the lack of diversity. Work loads can be more easily controlled as they can be more fairly allocated as the nature of the work is homogeneous, i.e. of a similar nature. Working methods and procedures can be standardised. Personnel have a limited outlook, however, as they do not see the job as a whole, only the part they are directly concerned with. This type of organisation applies to the grouping of capstans, millers and drillers in a factory into their own specific sections, etc. In the office, the grouping of typing services and reprographics as a central service for the administration as a whole also follows this principle of organisation.

Horizontal integration. The combining of several similar businesses to rationalise manufacturing and selling activities for economy of scale; the avoidance of uneconomic duplication of resources; the elimination of unnecessary competition and the provision of additional research and/or production resources, etc.

Horizontal relationship. *See* LATERAL RELATIONSHIP.

Human relations. The philosophy relating to the morale, social and psychological factors of people in their working environment. The philosophy has the welfare of people as its main consideration, particularly in attempts to thwart the dehumanisation of working environments due to the advance of scientific and technological developments. *See* ORGANISATION THEORY 3 and PIONEERS OF MANAGEMENT.

Human resources accounting. Normal accounting conventions do not provide for entering the value of human resources on the balance sheet, even though it is generally recognised that the people forming an organisation are the most valuable resource. It is said that omitting human resources from the balance sheet deprives shareholders and management of important information in respect of the workforce. It is, of course, normal accounting practice to account for expenditure relating to recruitment and training of personnel and all payroll costs, but not the valuation of employees as a business asset in the same way as plant and machinery. A business does not own its human resources—it only employs them.

Hygienes. *See* MOTIVATION THEORY 2.

I

Industrial Common Ownership Movement (ICOM). *See* WORKER CO-OPERATIVES.

Imperfect competition. A market situation containing monopolistic factors which allows for the application of undue influences to supply, demand and prices by buyers and sellers.

Incentive scheme. A scheme of remuneration based on some form of payment by results (PBR) (q.v.). There exist many types of scheme, some of which are of an individual nature such as piecework, and others which apply to group activities in the form of a bonus. Some schemes apply gearing techniques. The main purpose of such schemes is to increase productivity, decrease costs and increase the earnings of personnel. The work unit on which the incentive payment is based must be easily recognisable; work generally must be repetitive; work should be specialised; the payment must be closely related to the effort involved; the standard of performance expected should be reasonably attainable by the average worker applying himself to the task without over-exertion; it should be fair to the employee and to the employer and the basis of any computations should be readily understandable by all concerned.

Incomes policies. Many economists argue that the way to manage inflation is to have a state regulated system of prices and incomes control. Incomes policies are intended to keep wages, salaries and prices broadly in line with increases in production and productivity. Successive governments have attempted to devise voluntary, statutory, unilateral or covert incomes policies in the post-war period, but no matter what scheme has been tried they have always been subjugated to collective bargaining (q.v.) in the end.

Incremental cost. The additional cost incurred by the production of an additional unit of production, or the cost which would be avoided if one unit was not produced. The incremental cost relates to the variable costs. *See* MARGINAL COST.

Index number. A useful means of showing relative changes in values relating to costs, prices and productivity. A base year is selected which is given the value of 100. Variations in subsequent years are computed in relation to the base year. For example:

1982 base year – sales – £100,000 = 100
1983 sales – £120,000
∴ index number = 120

Indirect costs. Costs which cannot be allocated directly to units or jobs but which can be apportioned to units or jobs on some suitable basis, such as a percentage of direct labour, or prime cost or as a rate per labour or machine hour. Indirect costs include indirect materials (q.v.) i.e. cutting oil, grease, solder; indirect labour (q.v.) i.e. labourers, toolsetters, shop clerks, chargehands; and indirect expenses, i.e. scrap, rectification, holiday pay, electricity (unless metered), overtime premium, depreciation of plant and machinery, rent and rates.

Indirect labour. Indirect labour includes those workers who are not directly identifiable with a specific job or products, but work for a department and would include shop clerks, sweepers, labourers and toolsetters, etc. *See* INDIRECT COSTS.

Indirect material. Material which does not enter into the product but which is used in the production processes generally such as cutting oil, grease and solder, etc. *See* INDIRECT COSTS.

Induction training. This is the type of training given to newly appointed personnel to provide background information on their new company, relating to management, organisation, products manufactured/services provided, welfare facilities, holidays, promotion prospects and where their duties fit in the overall scheme of things. It enables personnel to become orientated to the business environment of which they now form a part, the company's policies, objectives and practices. Induction training may also incorporate tours of the works, films of manufacturing processes and talks by managers, etc.

Industrial democracy. The philosophy of appointing worker/directors to enable the employees of an organisation to participate in its management. Rather than being in a passive role of acting on instructions from immediate superiors, employees are able to assist in the formulation of policy prior to its implementation. The philosophy should engender increased levels of cooperation in an organisation and as a result enable it to achieve its objectives more effectively.

Industrial disputes. These arise for a multiplicity of reasons and manifest themselves in a variety of ways. Most companies have developed procedures for dealing with disputes, but if these break down the common courses of action taken by employees are overtime bans, work-to-rules (q.v.) and a whole variety of restrictive practices, strikes (q.v.) or boycotts. *See* INDUSTRIAL RELATIONS.

Industrial dynamics. The interactions of business activities and the study of their cause and effect relationships as a basis for optimising the performance of the business as a whole and to attain a state of homeostasis (q.v.). The study is performed on a continuing basis and embraces the appraisal of material movements, cash flows, manpower mobility and the flow of finished products in the organisation. *See also* CYBERNETICS, CLOSED LOOP SYSTEM and CURRENT ASSETS.

Industrial engineering. The term is of American origin and is not widely used in the UK. It is often used as another term for work study (q.v.) but it has a wider meaning. It is a term which embraces the whole of a business, viewing it as a system. Industrial engineering is not restricted to manufacturing industries but also applies in public services. When related to manufacturing, industrial engineering views the activity as a total production system and is concerned with the design, development, improvement and installation of integrated systems, utilising resources in an optimum manner. It draws upon operational research techniques and industrial psychology (q.v.). *See* MANAGEMENT SCIENCE.

Industrial estate. Perhaps better known as a trading estate, they are government sponsored developments in under-developed areas. Factories, and the land on which they are sited, are available at low rates for new businesses. Many are well-planned, with imposing buildings that blend with the landscape.

Industrial marketing. A type of marketing concerned with selling goods and services used in manufacturing consumer goods. The customers in this case are not the final consumer. The marketing of machines and industrial process equipment such as electroplating plant would come within this category.

Industrial products. Those types of product which are purchased by a business to assist in the manufacturing process rather than being consumed directly by the purchaser. Sometimes the product, for example a microprocessor, may form part of the final product such as a washing machine, microcomputer or video game.

Industrial psychology. The study of human behaviour in the working environment. Different people react to various situations in different ways; indeed the same personnel react differently to the same situation at different times which leads to very complex studies. It is important to appreciate cause and effect situations as far as the human element is concerned, as it is the least predictable of all business resources.

Industrial relations. The relationship which exists between management, government and employees in the industrial environment. It embraces all environments where employees are remunerated for their effort, including factories, banks, shops and hospitals. The term is sometimes used in a curtailed way in relation to the collective relations which exist between trade unions and employers. The term is also used to cover formal aspects relating to collective agreements and rules relating to working practices. Industrial relations problems arise over disputes relating to bonus schemes, piece-rates or disciplinary measures taken by management regarding work allocations, suspensions, tea breaks (the duration of), etc. Industrial relations conflicts can arise at various levels; the level of the individual business in respect of local disputes; the level of a specific industry such as motor industry or health workers, and at government level when restricting wage awards to combat inflation. *See* INDUSTRIAL DISPUTES.

Industrial training boards. Government established training boards which have two main responsibilities: to ensure that adequate training is provided for its particular industry and to publish information on the training requirements of different occupations.

Industrial tribunal. A type of court comprising a legally qualified chairman and two lay members. They deal with matters of dispute relating to unfair dismissal, redundancy pay, and sex discrimination. Parties having a hearing may be represented by a solicitor or counsel, a representative of a trade union or any person of their choice. Appeals against the findings of an industrial tribunal are allowed.

Industry. In general terms, industry relates to all the businesses pursuing similar activities or producing similar products, i.e. those which belong to the same industrial classification. This includes primary manufacturers such as those in the car industry and their suppliers. The general classification of industries includes banking, insurance, hotel, catering, holidays (tour operators), shipbuilding, engineering and building, etc.

Inflation. An economic phenomenon which causes prices for goods and services to rise either through "demand pull" (q.v.) or "cost push" (q.v.) situations. This in turn generates a demand for further wage increases which generates further price increases and so the spiral continues. It is primarily due to too much money chasing too few goods, i.e. scarce resources. The economy gets over heated, pushes up the price of goods for export, which puts the country at a competitive disadvantage with other countries with lower rates of inflation. This then causes balance of payments difficulties. Restrictive wage awards assist in lowering the temperature and holding the level of inflation steady. This in turn increases the level of confidence in the economy which should generate additional demand and reduce the level of unemployment as a consequence. This is a simplified definition but indicates the nature of inflation and its effect on the economy as a whole.

Informal relationship. Those relationships which exist between individuals and groups of personnel in the same department, or personnel in different departments having similar interests, ideals, ideas and attitudes. Relationships which are not part of the formal organisation structure. The management of a business determines the formal relationships but individuals determine the informal relationships. Such relationships should not be ignored, as they have a bearing on the attainment of corporate goals. Dissenting attitudes will be obstructive in the pursuit of formal goals.

Information, management. Information which is used as a basis for planning and controlling business operations. Information is the lifeblood of business operations and plays an imperative part in the management of an enterprise. Up-to-date information enables management to respond to situations whilst they are current and not historical which is essential if corporate goals are to be achieved. Information provides the necessary ingredient of intelligence in respect of the external and internal environment, enabling management to make balanced judgments.

Information retrieval. The process of gaining access to information stored in information files and its presentation in a form suitable for its purpose. To this end, managers are often provided with a terminal connected to a computer giving access to information stored in a database on a random access basis. This facility speeds up the flow of information, thus improving the efficiency of a business.

Information system. *See* MANAGEMENT INFORMATION SYSTEM.

Information technology. The term generally relates to the harnessing of electronic technology for the information needs of businesses at all levels of their hierarchy.

The term "convergence" is often used to define the merging of various aspects of the spectrum of electronic technology. It embraces the use of microcomputers for information processing and storage, including the application of electronic spread sheets and business modelling programs, word processing for preparing standard reports and other correspondence at high speed, and electronic mail for transmitting information from one office or site to another without the use of paper by means of data transmission lines linking microcomputers or devices known as office information systems (OIS). Information technology also embraces the use of interactive "viewdata" database systems such as British Telecom's Prestel (q.v.) or private internal viewdata systems such as ICL's Bulletin. Such systems are interactive because after information has been accessed and displayed on the screen of a television the user can, for example, book hotel accommodation or order goods at a supermarket by means of a keypad which transmits the required information where it is stored ready for processing. Also included are distributed processing and information systems often organised as local area network systems which allow information interchange between different parts of an organisation whilst sharing central resources, such as a database supported by a mainframe, high capacity storage and high speed printing facilities. Many systems use twisted-pair wires or coaxial cable allowing data transmission speeds in the region of one million bits per second. The technology also includes the use of message switching and digital PABX facilitating both voice and data transmission, and the use of electronic printing equipment. *See* PRESTEL and TELETEXT.

Insolvency. The situation when an individual or company is unable to meet its financial commitments as they become due, because of a shortage of liquid resources.

The Institute of Chartered Secretaries and Administrators. The Institute is the leading professional body for company secretaries and administrators with the aim of efficient administration in all spheres of business and public service. Membership is attained on the basis of examinations and relevant experience. Grades of membership are Associate (ACIS) and Fellow (FCIS). The Institute has in the region of 44,000 members and 25,000 registered students worldwide.

The Institute of Cost and Management Accountants. The objectives of the Institute are to promote and develop the practice of management accountancy and is the professional body for cost and management accountants. Membership is granted on the basis of passing prescribed examinations, or specific exemptions from some parts of the examinations, and appropriate experience. The Institute has two grades of membership, Associate (ACMA) and Fellow (FCMA). Membership is in the region of 20,000 with 40,000 registered students world-wide.

The Institute of Management Services. The professional and qualifying body for people in work study, organisation and methods, and related management services, with the objectives of the creation of professional standards for the practice of work study, organisation and methods and other management services; the provision of a system of qualifying examinations; to ensure that professional standards are maintained, etc. The classes of membership include non-corporate and corporate categories. The non-corporate includes Affiliate, Licentiate and Graduate. The corporate includes Member (MMS) and Fellow (FMS). The Institute has in the region of 21,000 members.

The Institute of Marketing. The main aims of the Institute are the development and the dissemination of knowledge relating to the principles and practice of marketing and the provision of services to members and registered students. There are three grades of membership: full Member (MInstM), Associate (AInstM) and Fellow (FInstM). Currently the Institute has in the region of 22,000 members and 17,000 students. Its examination structure provides for the Certificate in Marketing Studies and the Diploma in Marketing.

The Institute of Personnel Management. The Institute is the professional body for those employed in all categories of personnel management and has qualifying examinations for membership although appropriate experience is also required. Membership is in the region of 20,000 and includes academics such as college lecturers in personnel management as well as practising personnel managers and their supporting staff. Membership is only available on an individual basis, i.e. corporate bodies cannot be members of the Institute.

Examination candidates are able to prepare for the Institute examinations in a number of ways according to personal preference. Most students study part-time at colleges of further education or opt for correspondence courses. Candidates for student membership of the Institute should be at least 20 years of age and have a minimum of stipulated qualifications. Regulations exist, however, which permit candidates not holding such qualifications to be admitted to membership. Five years' experience in personnel work is required for corporate membership of the Institute.

The Institution of Industrial Managers. The Institution represents those engaged in industrial management with the primary aim of increasing productivity by developing and improving the standard of industrial management. The grades of membership are Member, Associate and Fellow. Many colleges and polytechnics provide courses of study for their examinations.

Intangible assets. These are assets (q.v.) which do not physically exist but can be of extreme value to a business. Intangible assets include goodwill (q.v.) and trademarks. Goodwill is of value when it exists as it has a bearing on the valuation placed upon shares when a takeover is under consideration. Trademarks provide protection of the products dealt with by a business as they clearly distinguish them from others of a similar type.

Integration strategy. *See* HORIZONTAL INTEGRATION and VERTICAL INTEGRATION.

Intelligence tests. *See* SELECTION TESTS.

Interfirm comparison. The comparison of different firms' performance data within a specific industry to enable each firm to assess its comparative position. It provides guidelines, i.e. parameters (q.v.), for monitoring each firm's achievements. This includes the use of ratios comparing last year's performance with this year's in respect of operating profit/assets; operating profit/sales; sales/operating assets; operating assets/average daily sales; production cost of sales/sales; distribution costs/sales; administrative expenses/sales; material stocks/average daily sales; work in progress/average daily sales; finished stocks/average daily sales; debtors/average daily sales. The Centre for Interfirm Comparison was set up in 1959 by the British Institute of Management, in association with the British Productivity Council, in order to meet the requirements of industry and trade for an expert body to conduct interfirm comparisons.

Interest on capital. When comparing the operating costs of alternative capital investments with different levels of capital expenditure, it is imperative that the interest on capital be included otherwise correct cost differentials will not be included in cost comparison statements; this could lead to incorrect decision-making. If machine A cost £10,000 and machine B £11,000, then, using an interest rate of 10 per cent per annum, the interest on capital for machine A is £1,000 compared with that of machine B of £1,100—a cost differential of £100 per annum.

Internal audit. *See* AUDITOR.

Internal auditor. *See* AUDITOR.

Inventory control. *See* STOCK CONTROL.

Investment analysis. *See* INVESTMENT APPRAISAL.

Investment appraisal. This consists of a number of techniques for assessing whether capital investments on projects in respect of new plant or buildings will generate an acceptable rate of return when compared with alternative projects. The techniques used include discounted cash flow (DCF) (q.v.) including net present value; internal rate of return (yield on investment (q.v.)); pay-back method (q.v.); rate of return on original investment and average cost per unit of output. *See also* CAPITAL BUDGETING.

Issued capital. That portion of the authorised capital (q.v.) of a company that has been allotted. The whole of the authorised capital may not be issued initially but may be drawn upon when required for business expansion. It is pointless issuing more shares than necessary as it will water down the return on the investment of the shareholders. Both the authorised and issued capital are shown on the balance sheet.

J

Job. The term is used in two basic ways. 1. As a description of the activities performed by a person as part of his/her employment, e.g. accountant, wages clerk, or machine operator, etc. 2. The specific requirements of a customer, e.g. constructing a window frame, cutting a batch of glass to size or painting a house, etc.

Job analysis. The process of analysing the attributes and features of a job, and the conditions under which it is performed, as a basis for compiling a job description and specification to help in job evaluation (q.v.).

Job card. A record of time spent on various jobs by an employee and used for job costing. The time may be entered by the employee by hand or by a time recorder and provides a means of keeping track of how a person spends his/her time. The details are recorded on wages analysis sheets for subsequent transfer to job cost sheets.

Job classification. A means of grading jobs, usually of an administrative nature, based on the qualifications, skills, training, education and level of responsibility necessary to perform a particular task. *See* JOB GRADING.

Job costing. The allocation of direct costs to jobs and the apportionment of indirect costs on a suitable basis in order to compute the total cost of a job for comparison with estimates. Used occasionally as a basis for determining selling price. *See* COST ACCOUNTING and INDIRECT COSTS.

Job creation. *See* WORK-SHARING.

Job description. A detailed outline of a job specifying the attributes and factors involved in its performance, including mental requirements, physical attributes, working conditions, responsibilities, stress factors, etc.

Job design. This is the process of deciding on the content of a job in terms of its duties and responsibilities, on the methods to be used in carrying out the job, and on the relationship that should exist between the job holder and his superiors, subordinates and colleagues. Job design has two aims: first to satisfy the requirements of the organisation for productivity, operational efficiency and quality of product or service; second to satisfy the needs of the individual for interest, challenge and accomplishment. The overall objective is to integrate the needs of the individual with those of the organisation.

Job enlargement. Expansion of the tasks performed by an operative (as opposed to performing one limited task) as a means of increasing job enrichment (q.v.) in mass production environments.

Job enrichment. A philosophy concerned with making tasks more interesting and satisfying to the operative, when additional remuneration has reached a disincentive level.

Job evaluation. A technique for establishing the relative merits of jobs within a business in order to establish pay differentials, i.e. relative worth. It encompasses a number of methods including "ranking", involving the placing of jobs in order of merit using relevant criteria; job classification (q.v.) or job grading (q.v.); factor comparison method (q.v.); and points rating, whereby points are allocated to job factors, the total points determining the rating in order to determine its position in the pay structure. Whatever method is chosen, there is an element of subjective judgment which can lead to anomalies. Any attempt at formal evaluation is an improvement on no evaluation at all for job analysis is essential for obtaining sufficient background of the job under review.

Job grading. The classification of jobs on the basis of the attributes required to perform them. An alternative term for job classification (q.v.).

Job rotation. The process of changing an operative's tasks periodically to overcome boredom, on the premise that "a change is as good as a rest".

Job sharing. *See* WORK-SHARING.

Job specification. A formal description of a job embracing the following factors: (*a*) job title; (*b*) immediate superiors; (*c*) immediate subordinates; (*d*) responsibility for specified duties including: motivating and managing personnel, planning, coordinating, selection and training of personnel, personnel development, general administration of specified functions, specific assets controlled; (*e*) committee membership; (*f*) limitations to authority; (*g*) organisational relationships.

Jobbing production. The manufacture of small batches of products, components or processing operations, such as electroplating, particularly as special orders to customer requirements. There is generally no repetition of products or jobs, but as various jobs require similar basic processing operations general purpose equipment is used. Machines and processes are usually grouped by the nature of the operation performed, such as milling, grinding and turning.

Job ticket. *See* JOB CARD.

Joint consultation. A democratic approach to resolving problems of mutual concern to the employers and employees of an undertaking. It is a process of communication for holding discussions on matters relating to discipline, training, safety, welfare, health and working conditions, etc. Discussions often take place between the representatives of workers and management in Joint Consultative Committees or Works Councils. The committees deliberations are generally advisory rather than executive.

Joint demand. The situation which exists in the relationship between various products, whereby the use of one generates demand for another. For example, tea, milk and sugar; strawberries and cream; bricks and mortar (sand and cement); cars and petrol; cereals and milk; bread and butter, etc.

Joint venture. A venture undertaken in pursuance of supplying a specific service or product by two or more parties, i.e. companies or individuals. An example is BARIC Computing Services—a joint venture between Barclays Bank and ICL Computers.

Junior boards. *See* MANAGEMENT TRAINING TECHNIQUES.

K

Key factor. *See* LIMITING FACTOR.
Kickback. An illegal inducement by way of a financial payout from one person to another (or by a corporate body) in order to obtain a sale or contract unfairly.

L

Labour. This term may be defined in a number of ways of which the following are three examples. 1. A factor of production (q.v.). 2. Effort expended in performing tasks. 3. Manual workers of an undertaking.

Labour agreement. A mutually acceptable decision on a course of action between employers and employee representatives to modify, improve or eliminate specific circumstances.

Labour relations. *See* INDUSTRIAL RELATIONS.

Labour turnover. A term used to describe the termination of employment of employees in a business. A measure of labour turnover is the number of employees who have left related to the average number employed during the period expressed as a ratio:

$$\frac{\text{Number of employees left during the period}}{\text{Average number employed during the period}} \times 100$$

The average number may be computed by simply taking the average of the number employed at the beginning and end of the period. It minimises the fluctuations which may have occurred during the period.

Laissez-faire management style. This may be defined as management by abdication, as no direction is provided to subordinates, who do as they please. This style of management may be due to managers being afraid to give appropriate orders.

Lateral relationship. Relationships which exist between executives having the same degree of responsibility and authority. This relationship may also exist between personnel, in the same department but having different supervisors but a common manager. When this relationship is in operation it should be with the knowledge of individual supervisors. The Scalar Principle, or chain of command (q.v.) is still in force under these circumstances. The same principles apply when extended to executives in different departments who are responsible to a common superior. These are day-to-day relationships which have as their objective the speedy execution of work and a shortening of the formal lines of communication. The technique is attributed to Henri Fayol.

Lateral thinking. This concept was originated by Edward de Bono who says there are two basic ways of thinking: (*a*) vertical thinking which is the conventional logical process; and (*b*) lateral thinking which deliberately avoids the direct logical path and is a different more creative way of using the mind. De Bono has developed techniques for breaking away from conventional patterns of thought thereby enhancing the mind's natural creative abilities as an aid to problem solving (q.v.) and producing new ways of looking at things and new ideas.

Law of diminishing returns. This is a well-known economic law which, in general, states that each successive application of a unit of a factor of production (q.v.), when combined with a fixed portion of other factors, will not increase the yield by an equal amount after a specific point has been reached. If one considers the application of fertiliser to an area of land, then there is a limit to the additional yield which can be obtained from additional applications of fertiliser.

Law of supply and demand. An economic law which is based on the theory that the price of products, goods and services are fixed by the interaction of supply and demand. The law intimates that an increase in supply will generate a decrease in price providing there is not a similar increase in demand. The reasoning is that in order to sell all of the increased supply, the price must be reduced to attract additional buyers. Similarly, a decrease in supply, providing demand remains constant, will push up the price creating inflationary tendencies.

Law of the situation. The law of the situation was evolved by Mary Parker Follett, an American who was one of the first to realise the part psychology has to play in the understanding of the behaviour of management and workers. In accordance with the law workers need to be able to perceive a justifiable reason for the orders given to them by a superior, i.e. they need to appreciate that it is the objective requirements of the situation which give rise to the order, not merely the superior's whim to impart authority.

Lead time. The time that elapses between placing an order for goods and the time they are received. The lead time may be a very short time for standard items available from stock, but for complex specials, having to go through stages of design, tooling, production and despatch, the lead time can be of considerable length. It is necessary for stock items to be held in such quantities that there is sufficient to satisfy requirements during the whole of the lead time.

Leadership. *See* DIRECTING.

Lease or buy. Alternative ways for acquiring the use of assets include leasing or outright purchase. Leasing involves the hiring of assets for a stated time by the payment of rental charges which are allowable for taxation purposes. The assets can be replaced after the leasing term has expired which is beneficial for keeping up-to-date and efficient. If assets are purchased this involves capital expenditure which may create a cash flow problem unless a bank or other loan is obtained to finance the asset in question. Loans attract high interest rates of course but they are allowable for taxation purposes. Depreciation allowances can also be claimed for taxation purposes which has the effect of reducing the net cost.

Leaseback. A means of obtaining funds with which to finance business operations or expansion when a company owns its own buildings. The buildings are sold to a finance or property company while the business retains the use of them by leasing them back from the purchaser.

Leasing. Leasing involves the hiring of assets by paying rental charges. The main advantage is that capital expenditure is not incurred which reduces the pressure on liquid resources needed for more important investments, and helps avoid the need to negotiate bank loans or overdrafts. Tax allowances are obtained on the rental charges. The assets acquired on lease never become the property of the business.

Levels of management. The management structure, or hierarchy, of a business consists of different levels of management because of the need to organise activities into functions, departments and sections for optimising the span of control. The purpose of this is to achieve the most effective command structure for the achievement of business objectives.

See HIERARCHICAL ORGANISATION STRUCTURE.

Liabilities. *See* CURRENT LIABILITIES.

Limited liability. The shareholders of a limited company are only liable for the debts of the company to the amount of capital they have agreed to subscribe. *See* COMPANY and UNLIMITED LIABILITY.

Limiting factor. The factor which will limit the activities of a business; a constraint to a specific course of action which is often the level of demand for the products or services of the business; or a shortage of one of the productive resources, e.g. skilled labour, raw material, or machine capacity. The extent of the influence of the limiting factor must be assessed before planning business activities. Limiting factor is also known as key factor or principal budget factor. *See* CONTRIBUTION PER UNIT OF LIMITING FACTOR.

Line and staff organisation. Perhaps more appropriately defined as line and functional organisation, because even though there are purely staff positions in an organisation, i.e. advisers, specialist functions predominate. Therefore, a line and functional organisation is one whereby specialist advisers, in the form of functional managers, assist the line managers in the performance of their responsibilities. The term line managers is probably a little outmoded as functional managers are also line managers having line authority over their subordinates. Line management (q.v.) traditionally referred to the production and marketing functions as they were the prime activities supported by staff advisers. In many instances, staff advisers are now attached to key functions such as management services, accounting services, purchasing and stock control, production planning and control and quality control. These functions leave line managers free to concentrate their energies on main tasks without being encumbered by administrative routine, relating to accounting, purchasing, work measurement, stock control, planning production and controlling quality, etc.

Linear programming. An operational research technique which assists in the solution of allocation problems of a linear nature. One application is the optimisation of transportation costs when supplying goods to various customers at different locations from dispersed warehouses. The aim is to optimise the total distance travelled to minimise distribution costs. Solutions to this type of problem can be obtained mathematically or graphically, with the aim of minimising costs or maximising profits by assigning limited resources in the most effective way. Other applications are in the formulation of recipes whilst attaining a specific calorific value, and for optimising production and profit with constraints on machine running hours available.

Line management. Managers responsible for controlling a specific business function are generally known as line managers as they have executive authority over subordinates within a formal chain of command (q.v.). Direct lines of authority are clearly indicated which also specify the formal communication paths within a business. *See* HIERARCHICAL ORGANISATION STRUCTURE.

Line organisation. A non-specialist type of organisation whereby managers perform a variety of tasks which would be performed by specialists in a line and staff (functional) organisation. In all but the smaller business, line managers can become overburdened by too many diverse functions: the most efficient of managers have their limitations, mainly due to a multitude of pressures. *See* LINE AND STAFF ORGANISATION.

Line relationship. *See* LINE MANAGEMENT and CHAIN OF COMMAND.

Lines of credit. The permissible amount a client is allowed to borrow from a specific source such as a bank.

Liquid asset ratio. *See* LIQUIDITY RATIO.

Liquid assets. Those assets which are either in the form of cash or which can be quickly converted to cash such as debtors, i.e. amounts owed by customers. A high proportion of current assets are in the form of raw material and work in process stocks which are not very liquid, particularly when production cycles are lengthy. This can cause a liquidity problem as current liabilities (q.v.), in the form of amounts owing to suppliers and the current tax bill, have to be met from current assets.

Liquidation. The process of winding up a business, perhaps as a result of unprofitable operations, by selling disposable assets for the best possible price to pay off creditors and other liabilities. Any surplus is paid to the owners or shareholders. The two usual methods are compulsory and voluntary liquidation.

Liquidity ratio. Sometimes referred to as acid test or liquid asset ratio. It is computed by extracting from the balance sheet the liquid and near liquid current assets and relating them to the total of current liabilities in the following way:

$$\text{Liquidity ratio} = \frac{\text{Debtors + Bank cash + Cash in hand}}{\text{Total current liabilities}}$$

The ratio should be at least 1:1 indicating that the liquid assets are at least equal to the current liabilities, enabling them to be discharged.

Listing technique. A problem solving technique which ensures that no factors have been overlooked when analysing the nature of a problem. It enables courses of action to be taken if specific events occur. Probabilities may be applied to the factors listed.

Loan capital. *See* CAPITAL.

Lock out. The prevention of employees entering their place of employment, because of action taken by the management of the business, due to some infringement of company regulations.

Long-term planning. Planning future business operations five to twenty years ahead is essential in some industries; for example, planning programmes for future timber requirements or for conducting searches for oil or other minerals of a scarce nature. Long-term planning indicates the future position if current results are projected into the future and if no action is taken to alter the situation. Such projections enable shortfalls to be assessed and suitable plans made to close the strategic gap (q.v.), as it is called, in order to achieve specific objectives such as a stated return on capital employed, or a particular growth rate of sales.

Loss leader. An item in a store or supermarket which is sold at a loss in order to increase turnover of other products. Low priced items may induce people to the store who may then also purchase other items. The store or supermarket suffers a loss of markup but offsets this by a greater volume of sales overall, and earns higher profits as a result.

Low geared. *See* GEARING.

M

McClelland, G. *See* MOTIVATION THEORY.

McGregor, D. *See* MOTIVATION THEORY 6, THEORY X and THEORY Y.

Machine hour rate. A rate computed for the absorption of manufacturing overheads related to operations performed on specific classes of machine. It is computed as follows:

Machine hour rate =

$$\frac{\text{Budgeted overhead cost of machine or group of similar machines}}{\text{Budgeted or normal working hours}}$$

This type of computation is a more accurate method of charging overheads to jobs as it takes into account the cost differentials for operating different classes of machines.

Management. 1. The expression "the management" relates to the personnel of the organisation charged with the responsibility of running the business efficiently within the framework of company policy. 2. The management of a limited company is the board of directors consisting of both executive and non-executive directors. The executive directors assist in formulating policy with the other members of the board but they also have day-to-day responsibility for managing a major function of the business. This is often achieved via their subordinates known as functional managers to whom they have delegated responsibility and authority. A typical board of directors of a manufacturing and marketing oriented business consists of a works director, technical director, marketing director, financial director and personnel director, etc. 3. The term management also refers to the activity of managing resources and the tasks of others in order to achieve defined objectives.

However, to define the activity of management fully, its definition should be expanded to embrace the following factors: (*a*) Good management must be forward-looking to detect threats and opportunities in order to either minimise effects or to take advantage of favourable circumstances. Management must respond dynamically to changes in the environment to ensure the business not only continues to exist but does so profitably. (*b*) Management embraces the planning of business operations to provide guidelines for future action in the pursuit of specific goals; the organisation of personnel to achieve tasks in the most effective manner; delegating, directing and motivating personnel in specialist functions to achieve objectives; controlling activities to ensure objectives are achieved or to modify objectives as circumstances dictate; coordination of diverse activities to avoid suboptimisation of corporate achievements; solving business problems efficiently on the basis of the correct facts and making the right decision at the right time. (*c*) Management may also be defined as the art of dealing with people, i.e. people management. F.W. Taylor advocated management by facts and measurement rather than by guesswork. Galileo stated that we should count what is countable, measure what is measurable and what is not measurable make measurable.

Management accountant. An accountant concerned mainly with providing management with periodic control information in the form of variances from budget or standard as a basis for taking action to achieve objectives, e.g. defined levels of performance in respect of overhead expenditure, production costs, labour efficiency, material utilisation, etc. He is responsible for all management accounting activities including the assessment of capital investment proposals, standard costing (q.v.) and cash flow analysis, etc. *See* MANAGEMENT ACCOUNTING.

Management accounting. The preparation and presentation of accounting and control information in a form which assists management in the formulation of policies, planning, control and decision making. Management accounting procedures include the analysis of cash flows, the preparation of budgets and operating statements, standard costing (q.v.), the preparation of periodic profit and loss accounts and balance sheets as well as the preparation of capital expenditure budgets, and the evaluation of projects including the application of discounted cash flow (q.v.), etc. These techniques ensure that managers are supplied with the information they need to guide them in achieving objectives for the operations for which they are accountable. Management accounting also provides variances and control ratios relating to overhead expenditure, liquidity and utilisation of resources.

Management audit. A type of audit concerned with reviewing the adequacy and effectiveness of the management structure, working relationships, utilisation of personnel and succession planning programmes, etc. It is often carried out by management services personnel such as organisation and methods staff. In addition, the audit should cover such matters as the effectiveness of the span of control of various managers, adequacy of the lines of communication, duplication of responsibility, the purpose and objectives of each element of the organisation being clearly defined, the extent of specialisation implemented, whether decisions are taken at the most suitable level, etc. Such a survey is essential in the larger company to ensure that the management structure accords with current needs rather than outdated historical circumstances.

Management by exception. A technique of management whereby corrective action is applied to the exceptions, i.e. variations from standard quality or cost; variations in sales quantities of various products; specific customers exceeding credit limits; stock items requiring replenishment and specific orders falling behind schedule, etc. The application of the technique improves management effectiveness as managers are able to concentrate on important aspects of business operations to the exclusion of others. *See* CLOSED LOOP SYSTEM, EXCEPTION REPORTING and CYBERNETICS.

Management by objectives (MBO). A management technique whereby managers participate in the setting of targets and ensure their achievement on the basis of formal job specifications which specify key result areas. This ensures managers know precisely what is expected of them. The essential stages of implementing MBO may be summarised as follows: (*a*) board of directors define corporate objectives; (*b*) analysis of management tasks by formal job specification defining key result areas and formal responsibilities for the establishment of objectives and the decisions to be taken by individuals; (*c*) setting of performance standards; (*d*) agreement of established targets; (*e*) coordination of individual targets with company objectives to ensure the achievement of optimum results; (*f*) provision of control information to managers periodically to enable them to compare results with targets and set new targets when necessary; (*g*) action effected to ensure the achievement of plans; (*h*) review of managers' performance by superiors to ensure that key result areas are being achieved; (*i*) development of managers by suitable education and training; (*j*) assessment of each manager's potential for promotion or other tasks; (*k*) review of each manager's salary. A constituent element of MBO is budgetary control which also provides for management participation in the setting of targets as a basis for establishing the accountability of managers. *See* MANAGEMENT DEVELOPMENT 3.

Management committee. A group of personnel with responsibility for discharging a managerial function or activity. A notable example is the board of directors which is a policy formulating committee and decision-making body. A data processing steering committee is another example, which exists for determining policy relating to the use of computers in the business so that their use is compatible with corporate strategy both for the short and long term. Management committees may also be formed for matters relating to manufacturing, quality of products and cost control. *See* COMMITTEE.

Management consultants. Specialists in various fields of management such as work measurement, management accounting (q.v.), management by objectives (MBO) (q.v.), organisation and methods (q.v.), operational research, personnel management (q.v.), computers and so on. Such consultants may be engaged to conduct appropriate studies within the business or to advise on specific matters. For such services they charge a substantial daily fee. Although these services are expensive it is also necessary to consider the benefits they may provide, e.g. avoiding expenditure on a large computer when a smaller one will be adequate for its purpose; improving performance by the application of work measurement, or improvements to current methods and practices.

Management Consultants Association. An association of management consulting firms established in 1956. Its primary purpose is to ensure that management consultancy work is carried out to high standards of ethics and competence. An annual check is carried out to verify that member firms continue to meet the required code of practice.

Management development. The process of training managers for the purpose of providing them with sufficient knowledge and experience to accept authority and responsibility for specific activities and functions, and to attain optimum efficiency in their managerial role in the attainment of business objectives. It has been said that a manager should be fully conversant with three jobs— the post currently occupied, the one prior to this and the one above. This assists management succession as managers can then move up the ladder of authority on a planned basis rather than as an emergency measure, thereby avoiding drastic disruption in the chain of command. Management development activities can be divided into six areas. 1. Review of the objectives, plans and structure of the organisation and the implications of present weaknesses and future demands on managerial requirements. 2. Analysis of the present manpower resources and future requirements in terms of numbers, types, knowledge and skills. 3. Performance reviews to identify development needs by highlighting strengths, weaknesses and potential for promotion. A particular approach to performance reviews is management by objective (q.v.). 4. Ensuring that managers are given the chance to learn by a combination of on the job training, provision of career opportunities to broaden experience and formal training courses. 5. Planning management succession to ensure that suitable managers are available to fill vacancies and future new appointments. 6. Planning of careers to ensure that people of promise are given a sequence of experience that will equip them for whatever level of responsibility they have the ability to reach and to provide individuals with potential with guidance and encouragement they may need if they are to fulfil their potential and remain with the organisation. *See* MANAGEMENT BY OBJECTIVES, MANAGEMENT TRAINING TECHNIQUES, MANAGEMENT SUCCESSION, MANAGEMENT SUCCESSION PLANNING, MANPOWER PLANNING and CORPORATE APPRAISAL.

Management effectiveness. The achievement of superior performance from inferior circumstances.

Management information. *See* INFORMATION, MANAGEMENT.

Management information system (MIS). A system which provides all levels of management with relevant information for the control of their function at the most relevant time, at an acceptable level of accuracy, with the appropriate degree of privacy and at an economical cost. A computer is often used for providing management information, as it is capable of an extremely fast response when designed for interactive on-line processing, for on-line enquiries or for the real-time control of business operations. An essential requirement of an MIS is the provision of feedback (q.v.) i.e. communicating a system's measured output to the control system for the purpose of modifying the input of resources in order to attain a state of homeostasis (q.v.). *See* CYBERNETICS.

Management levels. *See* LEVELS OF MANAGEMENT.

Management of change. A management philosophy which enables a business to react dynamically to random disturbances in order to maintain a steady progressive course in the attainment of objectives. Accordingly, managers must always be forward-looking to detect situations requiring a need to modify existing plans, or to change current practice to optimise performance when operations are subjected to environmental influences, some of which are likely to become permanent such as inflation, recession and unemployment. It is imperative for managers to detect threats to the profitability or survival of the business; it is equally important for them to detect opportunities which are essential for its continuing profitability. It is essential to respond to these situations dynamically whilst situations are current and not historical. Many techniques have been developed to assist an organisation to adapt its resources, both human and technical, to changing demands. These include organisation development (OD) which in its most general sense is an attempt to improve the overall effectiveness of an organisation by means of change agents or catalysts. These may be internal or external consultants, work restructuring programmes, job enrichment programmes (q.v.), participative management, to name but a few.

Management of human resources. *See*

HUMAN RESOURCES ACCOUNTING and PERSONNEL MANAGEMENT.

Management ratios. Ratios assist the task of management as they clearly define operational relationships between activities and use of resources, and as such may be used as a basis for managerial control. The ratios may be used for comparing the achievements of one period with another, actual results with budget, standard costs with actual costs, for comparing one section of a business with another and for interfirm comparisons. *See* ASSET UTILISATION RATIO, CONTRIBUTION TO SALES RATIO, CURRENT RATIO, DEBTOR CONTROL RATIO and FINANCIAL RATIOS.

Management science. Usually refers to the application of operational research techniques, both of a quantitative and non-quantitative nature, to business operational problems. The objective is to optimise the use of resources in the most effective manner by the removal, as far as possible, of subjective judgment. It is essential first to recognise the type of problem to be resolved before attempting a solution; a **correct** solution to the **wrong** problem serves no purpose and, if implemented, could prove disastrous to the business. *See* PROBLEM SOLVING.

Management services. The function which provides services to management, and to the business as a whole, by investigating problem areas throughout the business and submitting recommendations for their solution. This embraces work study of both direct and indirect activities within the organisation, organisation and methods studies, computer studies and operations research type studies. *See* WORK STUDY, OPERATIONS RESEARCH and ORGANISATION AND METHODS.

Management studies. Studies which embrace all aspects of the managerial process including the art of management, management functions, principles of management, management science, pioneers of management, organisation theory and other related topics such as finance and cost accountancy. These topics form part of many college-based management courses, which are designed to provide the necessary background for management students and to enlighten experienced managers on modern techniques and philosophies.

Management style. The approach adopted to implementing the managerial task is referred to as management style. One could analyse style in a number of ways including: motivational style—getting things done by some suitable motivating influence such as monetary reward; leadership style—enlisting the aid of others on the basis of high-powered leadership, that is by example; monitoring style—ensuring that all activities are delegated to subordinates and close control maintained over their performance; do-it-yourself style—a manager endeavours to perform all important activities personally in the belief that the only way to get it done properly is to do it oneself. *See* AUTOCRATIC MANAGEMENT STYLE and DEMOCRATIC MANAGEMENT STYLE.

Management succession. A planned approach to the development of management succession paths in an organisation. It is imperative to plan for future managerial requirements in line with future strategy. Future expansion or contraction plans must be considered so that managerial resources can be planned accordingly. It is an on-going activity as no situation is static for long and managers are not born: they must be trained. *See* MANAGEMENT DEVELOPMENT.

Management succession planning.

The process of preparing managers to take over specified managerial posts in the future on a planned basis. This allows continuity of management when existing managers retire or are transferred to other posts. This may be achieved by appointing junior managers as assistants to other managers whose posts they are destined to succeed. This avoids haphazard appointments of a temporary or permanent nature, on an ad hoc basis. *See* MANAGEMENT DEVELOPMENT.

Management theory. The underlying body of knowledge relating to management including principles and concepts which provide guidance to the practice of management. It embraces the underlying consideration of cause and effect relationships which are used as a guide in the problem solving and decision making process. Some aspects of management theory have become apparent from experimentation and others from years of practical experience. Behavioural elements of management can be predicted on a probability basis when influenced by identifiable factors.

Management training. Managers are trained in a number of ways in order to fit them for their specific task. Methods include obtaining experience as a management trainee spending time in various departments to provide a broad base on which to build future experience; acting as under-study to a manager to gain experience but not necessarily for taking over that particular post (this may be supplemented by in-plant training perhaps conducted by visiting college lecturers); full-time management courses at colleges of further education and polytechnics (these may be on a sandwich course basis); attendance at conferences in order to be aware of current developments; short courses at various colleges or private management training organisations. *See* MANAGEMENT SUCCESSION, MANAGEMENT DEVELOPMENT, MANAGEMENT BY OBJECTIVES and MANAGEMENT STUDIES.

Management training techniques. Used as part of a management development programme, management training must be based on self-development. Managers and aspiring managers have a responsibility to develop themselves, to extend their knowledge and keep it up to date, to improve their skills and when necessary acquire new ones.

On the job training techniques, which are sometimes referred to as "action learning" are an important element of management training. Coaching can be given by existing managers, special assignments and projects can broaden experience. Junior boards, of which there are many variations, require its members to work as a team on a series of real problems. In some companies personal assistant positions are used for development purposes. Other possibilities of on the job training include guided reading, job rotation and secondment to other companies.

Formal management training programmes can be run by the company, by training companies or by consultants to fulfil a specific, identified need. Techniques used include: lectures; case studies whereby participants are given detailed reports of a business situation which is analysed and discussed; role playing which involves participants assuming roles and enacting them; business games which involve an exercise based on a business or a marketing situation.

Sensitivity training is used to develop skills in handling people. One technique used is the T group which involves small groups of about eight to ten people (with one or two trainers) who study its members' own behaviour and become a kind of laboratory in human relations. *Coverdale training* is a more structured form of interactive skills training. *Managerial grid training* as developed by Blake and Mouton consists of a simple diagnostic framework to aid participants to describe one another's behaviour in simulated situations. *Transactional analysis* is another technique used to develop interactive and communication skills in which the participant's behaviour in a variety of simulated and real situations is analysed using a prescribed method. *See* BUSINESS GAME, MANAGEMENT DEVELOPMENT and MANAGERIAL GRID.

Managerial economics. This class of economics includes the study of topics relating to costs, profits and investment geared to the individual firm in the real world, rather than mere theoretical conjecture of a general nature. It also embraces the application of operational research and accounting techniques related to problem solving and decision making. Economics is primarily concerned with the most effective use of resources, and this is also a primary role of management, aided by whatever branch of economics is appropriate.

Managerial grid. A management training technique aimed at providing managers with a clearer understanding of the methods used for achieving results through people, and the reactions of people to different management methods. The managerial grid developed by Drs Blake and Mouton concentrates on managerial behaviour. Attendance at a managerial grid seminar is usually the first requirement for this training technique. The grid assists in the evaluation of concern for people and concern for results. *See* MANAGEMENT TRAINING TECHNIQUES.

Managerial strategy. *See* MANAGEMENT STYLE.

Managing director. The chief executive of a company is the managing director, sometimes referred to as "the first among equals", meaning that he is the chief coordinator or team leader. It is essential for one person to be in overall control so that the elements of management can be implemented effectively. It may sometimes be necessary to have joint managing directors when the span of control is too great for one chief executive to manage effectively. In such cases, each managing director is responsible for major divisions of the business, but it is essential for them to coordinate with each other to ensure that a common course of action is pursued within the corporate framework.

Manpower budget. A budget for assessing the personnel requirements of a business in accordance with the anticipated level of activity, average level of performance and utilisation. The budget provides for all classes of manpower including managerial and administrative staff, direct and indirect operatives. If expansion is envisaged then a manpower budget provides the details required to enable a recruitment campaign to be undertaken. If the present establishment of personnel exceeds current requirements in specific departments, then inter-departmental transfers may be affected. Unfortunately, redundancy may be unavoidable unless it is possible to reduce manpower to the desired level by natural wastage. Due to the specific circumstances prevailing in a business various levels of activity may be budgeted throughout the year in accordance with changing demand. Accordingly it will be necessary to incorporate the anticipated timing of increases and decreases as the situation demands.

Manpower planning. The assessment of the best use of manpower resources to achieve specific objectives outlined in corporate plans. The purpose of manpower planning is also to assess the number of employees to be retired, promoted and perhaps retrained, in accordance with changing technology and other economic factors. *See* MANAGEMENT SUCCESSION PLANNING and MANAGEMENT DEVELOPMENT.

Manpower Services Commission. The Commission came into existence to assess possible shortages of skilled manpower and the provision of training facilities to improve employment prospects. The Commission operates through three divisions—employment, training services and special programmes for unemployed youths and adults.

Marginal cost. The variable cost incurred during the manufacture of a single unit of product or output, i.e. the sum of prime cost and variable overheads. The variable cost remains constant per unit, regardless of the level of activity attained, conversely, it is the cost that will not be incurred if a unit of production is not produced. Fixed costs are not allocated to products but charged in the accounts as a periodic charge. *See* UNIT COST and VARIABLE COSTS.

Margin of safety. The excess of actual sales over the break-even level of sales, e.g. if a business is analysed as follows then the margin of safety can be computed:

	£
Sales 10,000 units @£5.00 per unit	= 50,000
Marginal cost 10,000 units @£2.50 per unit	= 25,000
Contribution £2.50 per unit	= 25,000
Less Fixed costs	10,000
Net profit	15,000

Break-even units = $\frac{\text{Fixed costs}}{\text{Contribution per unit}}$ = $\frac{£10,000}{£2.50}$ = 4,000 units

Margin of safety = Actual sales − Break-even sales
= 10,000 − 4,000
= 6,000 units

This means that sales could fall to 4,000 units without sustaining a loss; therefore the margin of safety is quite high at 6,000 units.

Market development. *See* PRODUCT MARKET STRATEGY.

Marketing. The activity concerned with assessing potential demand for specific goods and services, the distribution of such goods and control of marketing resources to sell at a price which achieves an adequate return on the capital employed. Marketing embraces all those activities concerned with obtaining and retaining customers including market research (q.v.), sales promotion (q.v.), selling, distribution and after-sales service.

Marketing cost budget. The anticipated level of overheads expected to be incurred for the projected marketing activities including those incurred in obtaining orders, advertising, distribution and after-sales service.

Marketing management. The managerial activities concerned with planning marketing strategy; controlling sales, selling and distribution costs; the level of stocks to optimise stock investment to satisfy customer demand with a minimum of stock out situations on the one hand, and an acceptable investment in stock on the other. Controlling the level of service provided to customers, product profitability and assessing the effectiveness of advertising media. Ensuring that customer enquiries are dealt with efficiently and that effective credit control is implemented.

Market penetration. The market share achieved by the products and services of a particular firm. *See* PRODUCT MARKET STRATEGY.

Market research. The activity concerned with collecting, recording and systematically analysing market data for assessing consumer reaction, in respect of specific goods and services, as a means of determining needs. The most efficient use of resources is then possible in pursuit of business objectives.

Maslow, A. *See* MOTIVATION THEORY 1.

Mass production. The manufacture of standardised products in large volumes. This is accomplished by the use of flow lines, automated machines, material handling equipment and plant specific to particular processes. This type of production achieves economy in the use of resources, providing demand matches production capacity. It is a highly capital intensive type of manufacturing and is unable to remain profitable in times of falling demand. On the other hand, production can expand quickly in times of increasing demand. It is necessary to have effective preventive maintenance programmes to ensure a minimum of plant breakdowns which disrupt the flow of production. Fixed overheads are high and will be under-absorbed in times of cutbacks.

Master budget. The ICMA define a master budget as a budget that is "prepared from, and summarises, the functional budgets". An alternative term is summary budget. It is in effect a consolidated budget for the business as a whole, indicating income and expenditure as appropriate according to the nature of the business.

Material control. The activity concerned with organising the flow of materials and parts in a business. It involves not only the coordination of stock control, but also the assessment of material and parts required according to a specific production plan, taking into account scrap allowances and existing stocks. It also establishes for all items a reorder level, minimum and maximum stock level and the economic batch quantity: advises management in respect of stock losses, shortages, dormant, obsolete, reserved and free stocks. The technique also helps liaison between the supplies manager and management accountant on make or buy decisions.

Material handling. The activity concerned with all material flows within an organisation, including the receipt of goods from suppliers in the receiving bay in readiness for quality and quantity checks and their subsequent transit to the stores, or work in process. Ensures that work in process moves smoothly through the various processes and between various departments using the most suitable means, including overhead conveyors, gravity chutes, roller conveyors, cranes, hoists and fork lift trucks.

Matrix organisation. This is an approach to organisation design originally used by NASA and the aerospace industry which is growing in popularity. A grid or matrix of authority is established. Authority within functional departments, e.g. manufacturing, personnel, marketing, flows vertically; authority that crosses departmental lines flows horizontally. Typically the vertical flow of authority is exercised by functional managers whilst the horizontal flow is vested in project or product managers. The project or product manager is accountable for the success of a given project or product that must be processed through all or most of the functional departments. The project or product manager is thus the central co-ordinator for all activities related to a given project or product.

Similar principles apply to the development of computer systems.

Maximax rule. A decision technique which selects the strategy that gives the maximum profit. This seems to be a logical path to follow but does not take into account possible losses. This may best be explained by an example. Let us assume that a cycle dealer buys cycles for £20 each and sells them for £30. If the cycles are not sold within the same week he sells them for £15. This detail may be summarised as follows:

	Selling price £	Profit £
If sold within the week	30	10
If not sold within the week	15	– 5 (loss)

A pay-off table needs to be constructed to evaluate the results obtained for ordering various quantities of cycles and for varying demand.

Pay-off table (profits/losses)

Weekly demand	Cycles ordered			
	0	1	2	3
0	0	– £5	– £10	– £15
1	0	+ £10	+ £5	–
2	0	+ £10	+ £20	+ £15
3	0	+ £10	+ £20	+ £30

The pay-off table shows that the maximum profit is £30 which causes the cycle dealer to order 3 cycles without considering that he can sustain a loss of £15 if he does not sell cycles at the normal price during the week.

Maximum likelihood rule. A decision making rule for risk analysis which is based on the most likely situation after taking probability into account. Assume that the probability of demand for cycles is as shown below:

Weekly demand	Probability
0	0.2
1	0.4
2	0.3
3	0.1

If the above demand and probability factors are combined with relevant profit figures on the basis of £10 profit per cycle sold, then the following pay-off table may be compiled:

Event demand	Probability of demand	Profit	Expectation
0	0.2	–	–
1	0.4	£10	£4
2	0.3	£20	£6
3	0.1	£30	£3
	1.0		£13

On average the cycle dealer can expect (expectation) to make £13 profit each week. The safest course of action is to order 1 cycle each week as this has the highest probability of demand of 0.4. *See* BAYES' RULE, EXPECTATION and DECISION THEORY.

Mayo, Elton (1880–1949). *See* ORGANISATION THEORY 3 and PIONEERS OF MANAGEMENT.

Mechanisation. Mechanisation is the application of machines instead of people to manufacturing and administrative processes, to attain higher levels of productivity, because of the higher rates of output attainable by machines. Automation is not a synonym for mechanisation as automation commences where mechanisation leaves off. The use of machines without in-built self-adjusting control mechanisms for modifying their behaviour in response to environmental conditions cannot be classed as automation. *See* AUTOMATION.

Mechanistic organisation. This type of organisation is rigid in construction and is based on the hierarchical management structure. The organisation operates within the framework of procedural rules and directives, designed to deal with a specified range of situations. Compare this type of organisation with a clock which is designed to perform a narrow range of activities—that is, tick at a given speed and move the hands round the face of the clock at a given rate of movement. Even a clock has a regulator, however, so that its speed may be adjusted when necessary in order that it may attain its objective, that of giving the correct time. An organisation built on the same principles can only deal with preplanned routine activities and situations. In the real world random events occur which upset the best-laid plans. Accordingly, an organisation is required to be capable of dealing with them, hence the adaptive system (q.v.) of organisation. See HIERARCHICAL ORGANISATION STRUCTURE.

Memorandum of Association. A document which contains specific details of a company relating to the nature of the business, its name, share capital, that the liability of its members is limited and the location of its registered office, etc.

Merger. See AMALGAMATION.

Merit rating. A technique based on subjective assessment for evaluating the performance of a person doing a specific job, rather than assessing the job itself (job grading q.v.). The technique is usually applied to the assessment of administrative staff. It often takes the form of an annual review conducted by a departmental head, or section leader, for determining the worth of employees to the business in order to position them at the appropriate point on a salary scale. The assessment takes into account a number of factors relating to appearance, manner, degree of cooperation with other staff and superiors, initiative, quality of work, aptitude, skill, achievement of time schedules, timekeeping, ability to accept responsibility, etc. Points are allocated for each factor assessed and the total points awarded determine the point on the salary scale. See APPRAISAL.

Method. May be defined as the *modus operandi*—the way in which things are done. Before the best method can be determined a number of factors must be taken into account—the volume of work to be done, the rate of output required, quality of output, etc. It is then necessary to match these factors to the specification of various machines and further assessments made in respect of capital cost, annual operating costs and anticipated benefits. Selection of the most suitable method is a task for methods engineers in the manufacturing environment, and for organisation and methods (q.v.) staff in the administrative environment. The selection of the most suitable method has a direct bearing on the ultimate productivity and competitiveness of a business.

Methods audit. An audit which is performed in the administrative function for assessing whether the most suitable methods and procedures are in use. This is one way of ensuring that innovation and change are implemented as changing circumstances dictate. The audit is normally performed by organisation and methods (q.v.) personnel.

Methods engineering. See METHOD STUDY.

Method study. The study of jobs to ensure they are being performed in the best possible way, i.e. by the best method. The method may relate to the use of manual operations but this may be improved by the use of jigs and fixtures to aid the handling of work. The choice of machine often depends upon the quantity to be manufactured. One-offs may be produced on a centre lathe, for instance, whereas batches of similar parts may be produced on a capstan (semi-automatic) and large quantities on an automatic machine. The unit time becomes progressively lower, the higher the quantity, because of the more efficient method used. The basic steps in method study are: select the job to be studied, record the details of the job and method employed, examine the details critically, develop improved method, install new method and maintain new method, i.e. review it periodically to provide for changing circumstances. The initial letter of each of the steps indicated spell out the mnemonic SREDIM or MIDERS when the letters are reversed.

Middle management. Managers of departments who are positioned between the senior management level in charge of functions and supervisory, first line, management. Depending upon the nature and size of a business examples include production manager, works engineer, sales manager, production controller, quality controller, industrial relations officer, stock controller, work study manager and computer operations manager. *See* HIERARCHICAL ORGANISATION STRUCTURE.

Minimax rule. The selection of an alternative strategy for risk analysis which minimises the maximum possible loss. The strategy is one of caution which rarely provides positive results. In the example of the cycle dealer used above (*see* MAXIMAX RULE,) the pay-off table shows losses of 0, £5, £10 and £15 respectively for orders of 0, 1, 2 and 3 cycles. The dealer will attempt to minimise his loss by not ordering any cycles. Therefore, he goes out of business because, even though he does not make a loss, he does not make any profit either.

Mixed economy. A type of economy which exists in the UK whereby private enterprise and nationalisation coexist. The economy consists of private and limited companies and nationalised industries like steel, shipbuilding, air travel and telecommunications.

Model. *See* BUSINESS MODEL.

Modelling package. Programs to run on a computer which are designed for business and financial planning, including cash flow analysis, profit and loss projections, etc. A well known package for use on microcomputers is Visicalc which allows the user to create an electronic worksheet on the video screen for recording details of the problem and on which results of computations are recorded. Such packages have "What if?" facilities which allows the results of adjusting specific variables to be speedily computed so that it is possible to isolate the effect on profits or cash flow of differences such as the level of activity and different selling prices, etc. This is known as sensitivity analysis.

Monetarism. A government policy which is used to regulate economic activity for controlling inflation by the process of curtailing price increases and wage awards and by cut-backs in government spending. It also includes the control of interest rates to maintain the value of the pound, and when rates are reduced industry can obtain funds at lower interest rates for business operations or plant replacement.

Monopoly. The control over the supply and price of a commodity or service by one business having a competitive advantage. Very often competition does not exist at all, as is the case with the gas, electricity and water service industries. There are no alternative sources of supply so the consumer must accept prevailing prices. Prices are monitored, however, by consumer watchdog organisations.

Monte Carlo techniques. As the name implies events in a system occur on a random basis by pure chance and it is impossible to predict events precisely in the same way that it is not possible to predict which side of a die will arise on each occasion it is thrown. It is possible, however, to assess the probability of which side of a die will be thrown in the long run. In business systems of a highly probabilistic nature, the only way in which the behaviour of a system can be predicted is by simulation. This requires the collection of historical operating data which is subjected to random selection by random number tables, or computer generated random numbers, to remove any bias from assessments. This may be applied when it is required to know the likely behaviour of a stock control system when subjected to randomness within variables such as variability of lead time (q.v.). The number of times maximum permissible stock levels are exceeded, and the number of times (occasions) items are out of stock, etc.

Moonlighting. Otherwise known as the "black labour market" or double job holding, this is the practice of having more than one job. Skill shortages or the shorter working week could encourage more participation in secondary occupations but could also increase levels of unemployment. In view also of the growth of part time working double jobholders could increasingly become a key component in manpower supply.

Motivation theory. Considerable research has been devoted to the study of work motivation. This research has resulted in important insights into what motivates people but it has also resulted in a very large number of theories vying for attention as the best explanation of human behaviour. It is quite likely that all motivation theories taken together predict most human behaviour but it is often difficult to specify the situation in which a particular motivation theory will predict individual work motivation. The most popular motivation theories are as follows.

1. *Maslow's "Hierarchy of Needs"*. The theory assumes that human behaviour occurs when people try to satisfy their unsatisfied needs. Needs, according to Maslow, are arranged hierarchically and that needs low in the hierarchy must be largely satisfied before needs further up the hierarchy will motivate behaviour. Physiological needs, the need for safety and security, the need to belong or social needs, the need for esteem and status or ego, and the need for self-actualisation form the hierarchy.

2. *Herzberg's "Two Factor Theory"*. Based upon unstructured interviews with 200 engineers and accountants Herzberg concluded that one group of factors called "motivators" caused job satisfaction and another group of factors called "hygienes" caused job dissatisfaction. "Motivators" are generally related to job content and include achievement, recognition, advancement, responsibility, the work itself and possibility of growth. "Hygienes" are generally related to job context and include salary, job security, working conditions, status, personal life, and fringe benefits. In Herzberg's view it is possible to increase job satisfaction without reducing job dissatisfaction and vice versa.

3. *McClelland's "Need for Achievement"*. McClelland believes that people possess the need for power, need for affiliation and the need for achievement but that people differ in the degree to which these needs dominate their behaviour. Perhaps

the most distinctive element of this theory is the claim that the need can be learnt or unlearnt.

4. *Equity theory.* This theory is based on the assumption that individuals are motivated by their desire to be equitably treated in their work relationships. The basic equity proposal assumes that when a person feels inequity, he is motivated to reduce it and that the greater the felt inequity the greater the motivation to reduce it.

5. *Expectancy theory.* This theory, proposed by Vroom, in its simplest form, says that a person's motivation to behave in a certain way is determined by the outcomes the person sees as desirable and their belief that these desired outcomes can be attained.

6. *McGregor's "Theory X" and "Theory Y". See* THEORY X and THEORY Y.

Motivators. *See* MOTIVATION THEORY.

Multinational organisation. A company which has manufacturing or trading facilities in overseas countries for the purpose of distributing its products more cheaply throughout the world. Businesses operating in other countries create employment in those countries and increase the standard of living of the local population to some extent, as well as making the market more readily available for the business. The operating results of companies belonging to a multi-national organisation are consolidated at the head office of the group, i.e. the parent company.

N

National Economic Development Council (NEDDY). Formed in 1961, it is an organisation for planning the use of resources in order to improve their utilisation and to improve economic performance. It also engenders greater coordination between industries.

National Examinations Board for Supervisory Studies (NEBSS) Courses etc. These certificate and diploma courses are available at colleges of further education and provide training in many aspects of management including supervisory studies, computer concepts, production techniques and management; personnel management, stock control, catering, accounting, work study and other management and business subjects. The courses can be varied to suit local needs or specific industry requirements. Successful students can proceed from such courses to those of a more advanced level.

National income. The net earnings of a country's factors of production (q.v.) over a specified time, i.e. land—earnings take the form of rent, labour—wages; capital—earnings take the form of interest in respect of an individual's capital investments (such as bank or building society deposits), or in the form of profit from the use of capital to finance business operations.

Nationalisation. The public ownership of businesses of national importance to enable them to be subjected to government planning and control as an integrated industry for the purpose of achieving a greater level of effectiveness for the economic good of the country.

National wealth. The total value of all assets owned by the people of a country at any one time, i.e. stock of houses, goods, money, cars, machines, buildings, factories, roads and other structures, etc.

Natural wastage. The reduction of an organisation's labour force for other than reasons of redundancy, i.e. retirement on the grounds of ill health, death or voluntary termination of employment. Management usually have a policy of allowing natural wastage to reduce the work force to the required establishment level. This policy avoids unnecessary hardship to individuals. Unfortunately, in a recession it has not always been possible to reduce the labour force to the necessary level solely by the use of this policy.

Nature of management. *See* MANAGEMENT.

Need for Achievement. *See* MOTIVATION THEORY 3.

Net assets. The net assets are total assets less current liabilities (q.v.). This equates to the capital employed (q.v.) in a business which corresponds to net worth (q.v.) or equity capital (q.v.) which normally belongs to the ordinary shareholders.

Net current assets. These are the surplus assets which remain after deducting current liabilities (q.v.) from current assets (q.v.) which is equal to the amount invested in working capital consisting of work in process, raw material and component stocks, consumable items, amounts owing by customers and cash at the bank or in hand.

Net present value. *See* DISCOUNTED CASH FLOW.

Net profit. The surplus which remains after deducting from the trading (operating) profit the financial charges, i.e. interest on loans and overdrafts and income from investments. *See* OPERATING PROFIT.

Network analysis. A technique for planning a complex project which requires analysis into its various activities and events. These are recorded on a network analysis chart. The chart enables interrelated activities and the critical path to be observed. The critical path consists of those activities which form the longest route through the network. If any activity on the critical path is delayed then final completion time of the project will be delayed. The chart also indicates activities which have a degree of float (spare time) as non-critical activities can be delayed to some extent without delaying the final completion time of the project as a whole. Resources may be redeployed to critical activities as the need arises. Network analysis techniques are very similar and include critical path method (CPM) and program evaluation and review technique (PERT). *See also* CRITICAL PATH ANALYSIS.

Network analysis chart. *See* NETWORK ANALYSIS.

Net worth. The equity (q.v.) of a business consisting of share capital (q.v.) and reserves (q.v.) including nominal value of ordinary shares, capital and revenue reserves and unappropriated profit. *See* CAPITAL EMPLOYED.

Nominal capital. The authorised capital (q.v.) of a business as stated in the Memorandum of Association (q.v.).

Nominal value. The face value of shares which is often different from their market value. This varies with the profit earning achievements of the business.

Non-executive director. A director who is a member of the board of directors for the purpose of policy formulation, but does not participate in the day-to-day management of the business.

Normal distribution. A useful measure of dispersion whereby the values in a "population" (a term which means the whole of the sample being analysed statistically) distribute themselves normally around a mean value (average) which when plotted on a chart forms a bell shaped curve. The bell shaped curve is formed when the distribution of values is normal, i.e. without skewness and is known as the normal curve or normal curve of distribution. 95% of the population are included in the range $AM \pm 2\sigma$, $99\% = AM \pm 2.5\sigma$ and $99.7\% = AM \pm 3\sigma$. (AM = arithmetic mean.)

Normal curve. *See* NORMAL DISTRIBUTION.

O

Objective rate of return. Every business should control its operations to achieve an optimum rate of return, that is a rate of return on the capital employed (q.v.) which is adequate to satisfy the shareholders and which is satisfactory for the type of business. To attain this it is necessary to establish an objective rate of return with which to compare the actual return obtained. It is also necessary to ensure that all capital projects provide a return on the investment at least equal to the corporate rate of return, in order to maintain the desired overall return. If the return is lower than the target, operating results should be subjected to a post-mortem to discover assignable causes so that corrective measures can be taken.

Objectives. A business must specify its aims so that it is capable of steering a steady course towards them, taking corrective action when necessary to avoid obstacles. Its aims are defined as objectives and to achieve them it is necessary to establish short term goals. These may take the form of budgets indicating the targets to be accomplished in sales, production, stocks, expenditure, manpower, etc. It is essential that all functions and departments work towards the achievement of corporate objectives subordinating their individual goals to avoid suboptimisation of the business as a whole. It must be appreciated that managers and personnel in all functions work for the same business; therefore, it is pointless not to work towards the same ends.

Obsolescence. The loss of value suffered by plant, equipment and machines due to the introduction of new models which usually incorporate technological advancements. Obsolescence does not mean that plant and machinery have no further productive use. On the contrary, in many instances, they will have suffered very little wear and tear—it is simply that improved versions are available. It may, of course, be difficult to compete with companies equipped with the latest models which have superior performance.

Office information systems (OIS). *See* INFORMATION TECHNOLOGY.

Office management. *See* ADMINISTRATION.

On the job training. *See* MANAGEMENT TRAINING TECHNIQUES.

Open loop system. The basic characteristic of the open loop system is that it does not contain the element of feedback (q.v.). Without feedback a system does not provide for the sensing of measured outputs for comparison with the desired outputs. Consequently the element of control is missing. *See* CLOSED LOOP SYSTEM.

Open shop. A business which employs personnel not belonging to a union.

Open system. A system which interacts with its environment, either for the collection of information on which to base strategy, or for conducting business transactions with suppliers, customers, the general public, trade organisations, etc. Such systems adapt to changes in the environment in order to survive. Examples of open systems include man, biological, organisational and business systems.

Operating costs. These costs may be

defined as the day-to-day expenses of operating a business, excluding those of a financial nature, i.e. interest payments on loans and overdrafts. When evaluating a reduction of annual operating costs anticipated from a proposed method, only those costs of a direct nature which can be identified specifically to a specific machine should be taken into account. Costs of a direct nature include operating labour and expenses, maintenance costs, electricity (if metered), general supplies and interest on capital. General overheads should be discounted. Note: although costs may be identified as being of a direct nature in respect of a machine, they are in fact indirect costs as far as units of production are concerned.

Operating profit. The profit which remains after deducting from gross profit the costs relating to administration, finance, selling and distribution.

Operating ratios. *See* MANAGEMENT RATIOS.

Operating statement. A summary of operating costs (q.v.), variances, income and profit of the whole or part of the activities of a business for a specified period, including comparative figures for previous periods and the year to date. Some statements also incorporate operating ratios. Each manager or supervisor should be provided with an operating statement for the section or department (budget centre (q.v.)) for which they are accountable.

Operation. May be defined in two ways in the business context: 1. an operation performed on material to change its shape or composition; 2. the process of running a business or undertaking a venture, may be defined as a business operation.

Operational. The process of being operated or used, employed on a specific task, or taking an active part in some activity. A business becomes operational after it is incorporated.

Operational planning. The process of planning the activities and resources of operational functions regarding manpower, plant, machinery, equipment, materials and services for achieving a specified purpose and objective.

Operations research. *See* MANAGEMENT SCIENCE.

Opportunities. In order to survive or at least remain profitable, firms must respond to change in the most dynamic way which may require drastic action such as the shedding of old technology in order to introduce new. This is necessary to offset the technological advantage enjoyed by competitors. Firms need to be clear on the new direction they should take. Recent examples include menswear establishments switching emphasis from formal clothes to leisure wear; the sports goods industry appears to be set for expansion as the nation becomes more sports conscious; need one mention the electronics industry and microcomputers in particular?

Opportunity cost. The cost referred to in "opportunity cost" may not strictly be a cost in the nature of an operating expense, but the loss of benefit suffered by choosing the next best course of action. This is the cost of an opportunity forgone. Of course, there may be a gain in another direction from the chosen course of action.

Optimisation. The process of deriving maximum benefit from the use of resources within the prevailing industrial and economic circumstances. In respect of stock control (q.v.), optimisation may require stock shortages and maximum stocks to be minimised by more sophisticated stock control and demand forecasting (q.v.). Optimisation of conflicting situations needs to be implemented to maximise benefits to the business as a whole. For example, the production function wants to produce long runs and the sales function to get orders for any quantity, regardless of production economy. This can only be resolved by carefully appraising all facts and deciding on a philosophy to suit the case. *See* COORDINATION.

Oracle. *See* TELETEXT.

Organic organisation. *See* ADAPTIVE SYSTEM.

Organisation. 1. A term used as an alternative to business, company (q.v.), or corporate body. 2. It is also used to mean the structure of an entity, e.g. a business, that is the way in which it is organised. 3. The manner of organising resources to achieve a specific purpose.

Organisation analysis. An activity aimed at analysing the elemental characteristics and structure of a department, function, or a complete business in order to establish the communication relationships which exist, the operations performed, equipment used, methods and techniques employed. Only in this way is it possible to note areas for improvement. It is also necessary to note the flow of work and the space occupied by various activities. Its ability to contend with anticipated growth can also be evaluated. *See* ORGANISATION STUDIES.

Organisation and methods. Generally known as O & M. It is a specialist function serving the administrative functions of a business. It attempts to improve the efficiency and effectiveness of clerical and administrative procedures and systems and the control of operations. This is accomplished by the study and improvement of the organisation structure, usually at the operational level, and the methods and systems in use. Usually more time is spent in analysing procedures and methods than on organisational aspects. Resources are utilised in administrative activities in the same way that they are used in production operations in the factory. Therefore, it is essential that they are used as economically and effectively as possible.

Organisation chart. An organisation chart is a graphical portrayal of the formal structure of relationships, responsibilities and authorities through which a business aims at achieving its objectives. A chart may be considered as the circuit diagram of a business structure without which the organisation may be ill-conceived and unlikely to work smoothly. As business organisations are dynamic there is bound to be a time-lag between the physical reorganisation taking place and the record of it being charted; therefore, at best, a chart will show the actual organisation only at a precise moment in time. Organisation charts provide a means of recording existing organisations, proposed organisation, a means of communicating with staff, determining management requirements, and showing working relationships, formal lines of communication and authority. Their construction should be simple, without too much detail, the date it was compiled should be shown and it should have an identifying heading with the name of its originator. *See* ORGANISATION STRUCTURE.

Organisation design. *See* MATRIX ORGANISATION.

Organisation development (OD). *See* MANAGEMENT OF CHANGE.

Organisation principles. There exists many organisation principles among which are: principle of specialisation (q.v.) relating to the division of labour; principle of correspondence (q.v.) which states that authority and responsibility must be coterminus and coequal; principle of unity of objective (see OBJECTIVES) which requires all departments to contribute to the achievement of corporate objectives; principle of the span of control (q.v.) which indicates that when a business exceeds a given size it is necessary to delegate (this is also known as the principle of the span of management); the Scalar Principle of unity of command (see CHAIN OF COMMAND) which intimates that clear lines of authority should be defined, and the principle of responsibility (q.v.) which says that the responsibility of superiors for the actions of subordinates is absolute.

Organisation pyramid. See HIERARCHICAL ORGANISATION STRUCTURE.

Organisation structure. The structure of an organisation, i.e. a business, is recorded on an organisation chart (q.v.) which gives a pictorial representation of the real life physical structure of the business. This consists of the structure of relationships, responsibilities and authorities through which a business pursues its objectives (q.v.). The organisation structure also comprises the formal communication network of the business through which decisions and instructions flow downwards and reports flow upwards as feedback (q.v.) for managerial control.

Organisation studies. A study of the working relationships which exist between personnel, their respective responsibilities and level of authority. The main purpose of such a study is to determine the adequacy of the span of control within various parts of the organisation, types of decision and the level at which they are made, lines of communication, objectives of each section of the organisation, extent of specialisation, and the extent to which activities are coordinated. This is a narrower type of investigation than that involved in "organisation analysis" as it concentrates on matters of organisation only. See also PRINCIPLE OF SPAN OF CONTROL.

Organisation style. The philosophy on which a business is organised for arriving at control decisions and the effectiveness of business operations which, to a large extent, is dependent upon lines of authority, delegation, working relationships and the structure of working groups.

Organisation theory. The study of the structure, functioning and performance of organisations and the behaviour of groups and individuals within them.

1. *Scientific management.* The first school of thought was the scientific management movement fathered by F.W. Taylor, an American engineer who sought to develop ways of increasing productivity by making work easier to perform as well as methods for motivating the workers to take advantage of labour saving devices. Frank and Lillian Gilbreth made very significant contributions in the fields of time and motion study and sought to improve the welfare of workers. Henry L. Gantt studied habits in industry and Harrington Emerson championed standardisation. In Germany Max Weber wrote of machinelike or bureaucratic structures where activities were formalised by rules, job descriptions and training.

2. *Administrative management.* Paralleling the growth of scientific management was that of administrative management thought. Henri Fayol identified five universal

management functions: planning, organising, commanding, co-ordinating and controlling. Fayol also developed several principles of management as guides to managerial action. Other important contributors were Mooney and Reiley who further elaborated effective organisation principles; Lyndall Urwick who helped to gather and codify early thinking on management and organisations; and Luther Gulick who contributed much in the area of public administration.

3. *Human relations movement.* The third major school was the human relations movement. The experiments conducted by Elton Mayo, a psychologist well known for his industrial research, between 1924 and 1932 at the Hawthorne plant of the Western Electricity Company in the USA revealed that an organisation was more than a formal structure or arrangement of functions. The results of his research focused attention on the behavioural approach to management and he concluded that "an organisation is a social system, a system of cliques, grapevines, informal status systems, rituals and a mixture of logical, non logical and illogical behaviour".

4. *Systems approach.* The fourth school was the systems approach which sees the organisation as a total system of interconnected and interacting subsystems, all mutually dependent. Major contributors include Trist, Bamforth, Crozier, Galbraith and Likert. *See* TOTAL SYSTEMS APPROACH.

5. *Contingency theory.* The current school is the contingency theorist which sees each organisation as a unique system resulting from an interaction of the subsystems with the environment. The motto of contingency theory is "It all depends".

Joan Woodward (q.v.) in a study of a region's industries found pronounced evidence that a firm's structure was closely related to its technical system of production. Other contributors to this school include Lawrence, Lorsch, Pugh, Hickson, Inkson, Child and Mintzberg. *See* PIONEERS OF MANAGEMENT.

Organising. An element of management concerned with the organisation of resources and activities to ensure the smooth operation of a business entity in pursuit of its goals. Organising includes the structuring of working groups for specific tasks, delegation of responsibility and authority for specified activities, ensuring that lines of communication and authority are clearly defined.

Overcapitalisation. When a company has share capital in excess of its current needs for the efficient operation of the business, it is said to be overcapitalised. In these circumstances the profits are insufficient to provide an adequate return on the capital which has been issued. *See* UNDERCAPITALISED.

Overdraft. An overdraft is a facility for drawing extra cash when insufficient funds are available in the company's bank account to cover amounts withdrawn. This situation may arise towards the end of an operating period while awaiting remittances from customers. It is necessary to obtain permission for overdraft facilities from the bank before using this means of finance otherwise the bank may not provide the service in the future.

Overheads. Operating expenses incurred in respect of business operations including depreciation of buildings, rates, insurance premiums, indirect labour, materials and administrative and management salaries. *See* FIXED OVERHEADS and VARIABLE OVERHEADS.

Oversubscribed. A situation which occurs when demand for a share issue exceeds the number of shares offered. This can occur when a profitable business requires additional share capital for expansion.

Overtrading. A term used to define a situation which occurs when expanding the scale of operations at a faster rate than can be supported by financial resources. This often occurs when a sales campaign generates a greater level of sales for which supplies have to be paid and overheads, wages and other costs have to be met for which there is a shortage of funds. The inward cash flow is inadequate to service outward cash flow requirements.

P

Paper profit. A hypothetical profit until the situation which can create the profit is implemented. As an example, a business may be in a position to sell its machinery at a price in excess of its book value, i.e. its written down value, after providing for depreciation due to wear and tear. Of course, a business would not do this because the machinery is needed for manufacturing operations which themselves produce a profit, probably in excess of the profit which could be achieved from the sale of the machinery. Therefore, it is purely a hypothetical profit—a profit only on paper. A further example relates to the profit shown in the profit and loss account. The profit assumes that all customers will pay their accounts. This is not so; therefore, the profit shown is a paper profit because it will need to be reduced by the amount expected to remain unpaid and written off to bad debts.

Parallel running. A fail-safe procedure used when developing computerised applications. It requires the running in parallel of both the existing system and the computerised system until the latter proves adequate for its purpose. It is fatal to dispense with the existing system until the new one has proved itself, as disruption will occur in the event of the new system failing to achieve its defined purpose.

Parameter. A value used for controlling a situation. For example, in stock control the level of stocks and reordering procedure is facilitated by control parameters such as reorder level, safety stock, maximum stock and reorder quantity. In a credit control system the parameter is the credit limit; in budgetary control the parameters are the various budgeted levels of expenditure allowed.

Pareto rule or law. This is an important law for application in various spheres of business activity. The law states generally that many business situations have an 80/20 characteristic (sometimes 60/40, 65/35, etc. so 80/20 is only an approximation). For example 80 per cent of the value of items in stock is represented by 20 per cent of the items. The degree of control over the stocks may be reduced by concentrating control on the 20 per cent high-value items; the remaining 80 per cent can be controlled less stringently.

Parkinson's law. The law of "spreading the job out" as expounded by Professor Northcote Parkinson. He actually phrased it this way: "Work will expand to fill the time available for doing it." The Professor implied that the time available for performing a task will be taken whether or not it is actually needed. An unproductive state of affairs.

Partnership. Two or more people combine to form a partnership for carrying on specific business activities. A partnership agreement provides for the amount of capital to be introduced by each of the partners and the proportion in which profits and losses will be shared. There is no limited liability (q.v.) and partners are jointly and severally liable for the debts of the business.

"Passing the buck". A colloquial expression which implies over-active delegation by a superior to a subordinate of responsibilities belonging to the superior. This often occurs when a superior does not possess the requisite degree of knowledge or experience to fulfil his obligations directly. Passing the buck is a means of hiding the shortcomings of a superior—they are hardly hidden, however: on the contrary, they are quite obvious. *See* DELEGATION and "BUCK STOPS HERE, THE".

Pay-back method. A method used for determining how long it will take before the amount of an investment (cost of machine or process plant, etc.) is recovered by means of cost savings realised from the investment. The method is inadequate because it does not consider the earning capacity or cost savings achieved from the use of the machine after the pay-back period. It may be computed as follows:

$$\text{Pay-back period} = \frac{\text{Capital cost of machine}}{\text{Cost savings per year (before depreciation)}}$$

If, for instance, the capital cost of a machine is £5,000 and cost savings of £1,500 are expected then the pay-back period is three and one-third years.

Pay-off table. *See* MAXIMAX RULE.

Payment by results. Payment by results (PBR) schemes are primarily concerned with optimising operator performance, to achieve the required level of production efficiency and cost effectiveness, largely as a result of higher levels of output spreading the fixed overheads over a greater number of units and thereby reducing the unit cost. PBR schemes reward workers for extra effort so that they also share in the benefits of higher productivity. Piecework is widely applied on the basis of a standard time allowance for the performance of a job or operation, or on the basis of piecerates, i.e. monetary rates. Other schemes include measured daywork and a variety of bonus schemes.

Perfect competition. An economic term which states that the market price of a commodity cannot be influenced by the action of one trader or business, that full information is available to all concerned, similar products are sold by all businesses serving the same market, and no one business has an unfair advantage of the supply of the factors of production (q.v.).

Performance reviews. *See* APPRAISAL.

Performance standards. These may be defined as measures or yardsticks for assessing deviations of actual performance to that required (standards) as a basis for managerial control. Standards of performance apply to many specific circumstances and they embrace standard costing (q.v.) which is a system of cost control based on the measurement of variances from standard; quality control (q.v.) employs standards in the form of control limits which are specified on control charts; output or operator performance standards are established based on work measurement. These standards relate to deviations from cost, quality, output and operator performance standards.

Perpetual inventory. The continuous updating of stock movements is referred to as a perpetual inventory. It enables stocks records to be maintained in an up-to-date condition, so that the true stock position is always known for business control requirements. When an inventory has a great number of items, updating and stock reporting is facilitated by on-line computer systems. The perpetual inventory technique enables operating statements and periodic balance sheets to be prepared as the value of items in stock is always known.

Personal assistant. A man or woman Friday performing tasks for a superior who is then free to concentrate on more important matters. This is an "assistant to" situation rather than an "assistant manager" situation where the "assistant to" does not have line authority over his superior's subordinates. An "assistant manager" does have line authority.

Personality tests. *See* SELECTION TESTS.

Personnel audit. An audit mainly concerned with reviewing procedures relating to personnel matters such as assessing the suitability and effectiveness of the methods and techniques employed for personnel selection, the methods of job evaluation used, action taken to minimise labour turnover, criteria used for personnel promotion and assessing whether there are any square pegs in round holes.

Personnel management. Managing the human resources of an organisation is referred to as personnel management. It is concerned with establishing policy in respect of recruitment, selection, training, promotion, salary scales, job grading (q.v.) and merit rating (q.v.). It is important for personnel managers to generate effective and harmonious human relations in the organisation and to discuss problems with trade union representatives regarding wage awards and working conditions. Ensuring that adequate safety precautions are implemented in accordance with current legislation is also of importance.

PERT/cost. *See* CRITICAL PATH ANALYSIS.

Peter Principle. Half in jest, the Peter Principle contends that in a hierarchy every employee tends to rise to his level of incompetence. Each person is promoted for good performance until he reaches a level where he cannot perform well, and there he supposedly remains. A humorous rebuttal maintains that the principle may indeed be true but organisations can still perform satisfactorily because there are competent people who do not want promotion or are blocked because they did not go to college, or because of sexual or racial discrimination.

Picketing. A demonstration by members of a union outside the gates of their place of employment because of a dispute. The picketing is for the purpose of persuading persons to work, or not to work, according to circumstances.

Pioneers of management. The pioneers are the early writers, practitioners and management theorists who generated the basis for formulating a body of knowledge relating to management principles and theory. Of the many pioneers, three spring immediately to mind: F.W. Taylor, known for his principles of scientific management; Henri Fayol, renowned for his principles of general management and Mary Parker Follett, for her principles relating to human relations. Many more people have, of course, contributed to modern management thought and practice including Elton Mayo, Henry Gantt, Joan Woodward and Frank B. Gilbreth. *See* ORGANISATION THEORY.

Planning. This is a very important management activity which may be defined as the philosophical and logical thought processes applied for determining the most effective strategy, or tactics to adopt, to achieve a desired result. Planning in business needs to be a dynamic process taking account of the changing environment in which business operates. A business must be capable of responding to change and this is facilitated by effective planning providing it has a futuristic panoramic outlook rather than an introspective one. In general, planning is concerned with WHAT is to be done, WHEN it is to be done, WHERE it is to be done, WHO is to do it and HOW it is to be done. How it is to be done is a matter of tactics involving the planned use of resources, i.e. machines, equipment, manpower, materials, tools, finance and space (i.e. men, money and machines).

Plant replacement strategy. When to replace old and worn out plant is dependent upon a number of factors. Primarily it is a matter of economic necessity to ward off the threats emanating from competitors who are using up-to-date machines. It is not a matter of how long the machines will last; it is a matter of whether the business will remain in existence without modern equipment. To ensure that it does so it must have a defined strategy on plant replacement, especially when launching a major new product such as a new car model requiring an automated assembly line.

Policy. See COMPANY POLICY.

Policy making committee. See MANAGEMENT.

Potential reviews. See APPRAISAL.

Preference shareholders. A class of shareholder which has a prior right to the payment of a fixed dividend in preference to the ordinary shareholders. Preference shareholders also have preference to repayment of capital in the event of the liquidation of the company. See CAPITAL.

Prestel. This is the view data system of British Telecom. It is a computer-based information system providing both general and business information on a wide variety of topics. To use the system it is necessary to obtain a special Prestel-compatible television set which is connected to a telephone line. A numbered control pad is used to contact the Prestel computer via the telephone line. The control pad is used to indicate the specific *page* numbers or indexes required to be displayed on the television screen. The computer responds by displaying the required page interactively. As well as receiving information users can send messages both to each other and to information providers using *response* pages. These allow the user, for example, to order goods from a supermarket without leaving the house or office, book a hotel room or reserve a seat at the theatre. All this is done interactively which makes the system a very powerful communication facility. The type of information available from the database includes share prices, financial statistics and ratios, intercompany comparisons, data on the economy, weather reports, sports results and so on. *See also* INFORMATION TECHNOLOGY and TELETEXT.

Preventive maintenance. The organisation of plant maintenance by predetermined schedules so that essential maintenance is performed, ensuring breakdowns due to lack of adequate maintenance are minimised. The planning task, although time consuming, has considerable benefits such as greatly improved productivity and reduced cost of replacing parts due to less wear and tear. The technique also requires regular inspection to detect the need for repairs. It can also ensure the minimum of disruption by organising the performance of major tasks during holiday shut-down periods.

Price/earnings ratio. This ratio indicates the relationship of the market value of shares to earnings. The computation is as follows:

$$\text{P/E ratio} = \frac{\text{Market value of shares}}{\text{Earnings}}$$

If the market value of 500,000 shares is £1,000,000 and the earnings are £200,000 then, the P/E ratio = £1,000,000/£200,000 = 5, i.e. the value in relation to earnings is 5:1. As a general guide, the higher the ratio the lower the earnings per share.

Primary ratio-Return on operating assets. A ratio which establishes the earning power of business operations which may be compared with previous periods and different companies within the group or industry by means of interfirm comparisons (q.v.). The ratio is computed as follows:

$$\frac{\text{Operating profit} \times 100}{\text{Total operating assets}}$$

The operating assets exclude funds invested externally as well as intangible assets (q.v.) such as goodwill, trade marks and patents. For managerial purposes "capital employed" may be substituted by "total operating assets" as a basis for computing the return on the assets used in operations.

Prime cost. Prime cost consists of the sum of direct material, direct wages and direct expenses incurred during the manufacture of a unit of production. It includes those costs which can be identified to a specific product. Prime cost is an element of marginal cost (q.v.).

Principal budget factor. See LIMITING FACTOR.

Principle of correspondence. This principle states that delegated authority must be coterminous and coequal with responsibility in order to get work done. There must be the power to give instructions to personnel responsible for specific tasks. See ORGANISATION PRINCIPLES.

Principle of responsibility. A superior is ultimately responsible for the actions of subordinates when executing delegated tasks. The delegatee has extended authority emanating from his principal. See ORGANISATION PRINCIPLES.

Principle of specialisation. The activity of each person in a business organisation should be restricted as much as possible to the performance of one main activity. The purpose of this is to obtain the highest level of productivity from the available resources of men and machines. When a variety of tasks are performed by individuals, the total output is less than if they concentrate on one specialised task. The reason is that no one can be expert at all tasks; therefore the average performance is lower. See ORGANISATION PRINCIPLES.

Principle of the span of control. When a business exceeds a given size it becomes impossible for one person to control adequately all activities directly. It is, therefore, necessary for delegation to be implemented, with reference to the principle of the span of control, which states that no superior can supervise directly the work of more than five or six subordinates whose work interlocks. V.A. Graicunas emphasised the complexity of controlling more than a few subordinates because of the increase in the number of relationships that occurred for each increase in the span of control. Also known as the principle of the span of management. See ORGANISATION PRINCIPLES.

Principle of the span of management. See PRINCIPLE OF THE SPAN OF CONTROL.

Prior charge capital. See PREFERENCE SHAREHOLDERS.

Private company. See COMPANY.

Probabilistic system. Business and economic systems are of a probabilistic nature as they are subjected to random influences from the internal and external environment. It is this factor which prevents their state being predicted precisely; it is only possible to assess their probable behaviour as the effect of random variations or influences cannot be predicted with any great degree of accuracy. The state of such systems can only be defined within specified limits even when they are subject to control. For instance, stocks of raw materials and parts are influenced by changes in demand and variations in supply. Stock control systems are implemented to detect and control such variations on a probability basis. Production activities are subjected to random variations in respect of manpower availability, machine breakdowns, power failures and material shortages. Production control systems are used to control such situations. The quality of production varies randomly due to inconsistency in the quality of raw materials, human judgment and machine malfunctions. Quality control systems are designed to detect and correct such events. In general, probabilistic systems are of a stochastic nature as it is not certain what outputs will be achieved from specific inputs because it is not possible to ascertain what events will occur outside the direct control of a system.

Probability. Business activities are influenced by random events and it is necessary to assess situations on a probability basis so that the likely frequency of events is predicted from historical facts or by assumption (hunch). *See* PROBABILISTIC SYSTEM and MAXIMUM LIKELIHOOD RULE.

Problem definition. It is important to know the nature of a problem before attempting its solution. For instance, faulty production may be the problem but the reason may not be attributable to one cause; it may be due to a number of causes, because of the random behaviour of the production system, such as faulty material, inefficient machines (need replacing), inferior personnel delegated to key tasks (training need or selection of more skilful personnel). Each of the separate problems contribute to the main problem.

Problem solving. A major preoccupation of management is the solving of business problems relating to the financing of business operations, dealing with production delays, ensuring supplies of materials, that customers receive their goods on time, ensuring that budgeted levels of expenditure are not exceeded, etc. The expertise with which the problems are resolved is largely a matter of managerial experience assisted by the use of appropriate quantitative techniques. Such techniques include linear programming (q.v.) and queueing theory (q.v.), etc. It is possible to solve problems of a quantitative nature on a computer using problem solving packages incorporating the relevant technique. Of course, many managerial problems are not of a numeric nature (quantitative) but relate to people. Problems of this type can only be resolved by applying common sense, managerial skill and human understanding.

The scientific approach to solving quantitative type problems includes the following stages: define the problem, collect and record facts relating to the problem, establish factors relevant to the problem, i.e. variables and constraints, develop a mathematical or statistical model of the problem for analysis by appropriate technique, e.g. simulation, linear programming, queueing theory. Collect further data as required by the model, define objective and develop alternative solutions by statistical or mathematical analysis or simulation, probably using a computer. Select optimum solution by appropriate technique, recommend appropriate solution to management for implementation, implement solution and monitor results by comparison with expectations.

Producer co-operatives. *See* WORKER CO-OPERATIVES.

Product design strategy. Design strategy is for the purpose of improving the appearance, performance, durability and simplicity of operation of the product as well as ensuring its cost effectiveness. British Leyland no doubt had all of these factors in mind when developing the Mini Metro. It is important to be aware of what competitors are doing regarding product design, because this may be the motivating factor for improving the design of competitive products. Design strategy is of prime importance to the prosperity of a business; not only must products be functionally efficient, they must be aesthetically pleasing. This factor particularly applies to such products as television sets, music centres, cars, motor cycles and washing machines, etc.. *See also* CORPORATE STRATEGY.

Product development. *See* PRODUCT MARKET STRATEGY.

Product diversification. *See* PRODUCT MARKET STRATEGY.

Production budget. A schedule outlining production plans for a specified future period, usually one year ahead, analysed into monthly production budgets. The plans include details of the quantity of each type of product to be manufactured in accordance with the sales budget. Adjustments are made to allow for the level of finished stocks. The budget provides the basis for drawing up component part schedules and schedules of operations.

Production capacity. A measure of production capability which may be expressed in terms of units of product, machine hours or man hours. It indicates the amount of production which can be achieved with the resources available. When planning the use of capacity it is prudent to allow for contingencies and not plan to use the full capacity available. Otherwise when random events occur it will overstretch resources and cause bottlenecks. Factors to provide for include rush orders, power failures, machine failures, waiting for materials, faulty materials, labour stoppages, etc.

Production cost budget. The budgeted cost of production as outlined in the production budget. The budget should be analysed into prime cost and production overheads as a basis for comparison with actual costs. The budget would be based on standard costs when appropriate.

Production costs. The cost incurred in manufacturing products for sale including direct materials, labour and expenses, i.e. prime cost, and production overheads, i.e. indirect costs.

Production cycle. The production cycle embraces the stages from assessing the requirements of customers to the despatch of goods. In between these stages are those concerned with the purchasing of materials and parts and the conversion of materials to finished parts by relevant production operations. When parts are completed they are transferred to the work in process stores awaiting issue to the assembly department. Assembled parts are then inspected, packed and despatched. Specials may require designing and material schedules prepared before production can commence.

Production management. Personnel responsible for implementing production plans, including the allocation and control of the use of resources, i.e. men, money, materials and machines, and for achieving specified targets including volume, mix, cost, quality, performance. *See* PRODUCTION PLANNING AND CONTROL.

Production planning and control. This activity embraces the planning and scheduling of production based on sales forecasts by time period, and allocating resources according to volumes to be produced. The activity is also concerned with controlling production, including the issue of works order documentation, progress control, the comparison of actual achievements with schedules and noting significant deviations. Provision of control reports to works manager and production manager, including information on arrears, manpower and machine utilisation and material shortages.

Production volume ratio. This ratio is the number of standard hours of production achieved, expressed as a percentage of the budgeted number of standard hours. The ratio may be calculated as follows:

$$\frac{\text{Standard hours of production achieved} \times 100}{\text{Budgeted number of standard hours}}$$

The ratio measures the extent to which the budgeted level of activity has been achieved.

Productivity bargaining. This term lacks exact precision but the Royal Commission on Trade Unions and Employers Associations defined it as "an agreement in which advantages of one kind or another, such as higher wages or increased leisure, are given to workers in return for agreement on their part to accept changes in working practices or in methods or in organisation of work which will lead to more efficient working."

Productivity ratio. The relationship between resources used i.e. input to the production process, and the production achieved, i.e. the level of output attained. It is a measure of the effectiveness with which resources are utilised. Productivity is improved the higher the level of operator performance, the lower the level of scrap produced and the lower the machine downtime, etc.

Product life analysis. This type of analysis is for establishing the stage a product has reached in its life cycle. The analysis is often separated into four distinct phases, i.e. introductory phase, growth phase, maturity phase and decline phase. It is difficult to assess the useful life of a product because it is not always possible to read the mood of the market. Consequently some products will not exist for long if they do not "catch on". Yet others will have an unexpectedly long life, for example the Leyland Mini and the VW Beetle. The assessment of a product's life is one of conjecture because sales may be boosted by additional sales promotion in the short term. A company should strive to have products that sell themselves (such as branded chocolates, soap powder, margarine, cereals, etc) as it is essential to avoid incurring excessive sales promotion expenditure on a declining product. It is important for a business to know when to discontinue a product and when to introduce new or modified products. The replacement of a product should ideally take place just as it has reached its peak, because it can only decline from that point. If a product, which has reached its peak, can be replaced by an equally profitable product then the level of profit will be maintained—otherwise it will decline.

Product life cycle. *See* PRODUCT LIFE ANALYSIS.

Product market strategy. This strategy is one on which other strategies must be based. It is a strategy that is dependent upon a number of interrelated imponderables, i.e. uncontrollable variables, and the following factors must be reviewed in its determination: size of the strategic gap, economic tendencies, trend of inflation, trend of unemployment, trend of demand, extent of competition, changing tastes, cost of finance and political upheavals at home and abroad. Product market strategy may be selected from a number of strategies e.g., market penetration—selling more of the same products to the existing market; market development—selling the existing range of products in new markets; product development—development of new products for the existing market and creation of new uses for existing products for new markets; product diversification— development of new products for new markets. *See also* CORPORATE STRATEGY.

Product mix. The composition of products manufactured and marketed by an organisation. From a profitability point of view, some products are more profitable than others as they command a higher price for a lower consumption of resources. It is, therefore, ideal to define the optimum mix which maximises profit as far as market forces will allow.

Product planning. The estimation of potential markets and of sales volume, determining the level of costs for the potential sales volumes and other factors of an economic nature.

Professional and executive register (PER). Operates under the auspices of the Manpower Services Commission (q.v.) and publishes a weekly paper listing personnel requiring employment in various occupations. Provides a recruitment service in the same way as private sector employment agencies.

Profit. *See* GROSS PROFIT, NET PROFIT, CONTRIBUTION and OPERATING PROFIT.

Profitability. *See* RETURN ON CAPITAL EMPLOYED, PRIMARY RATIO, PROFIT TO SALES RATIO and CONTRIBUTION.

Profit and loss account. This is an account which is compiled at the conclusion of an accounting period for a business for the purpose of calculating the net profit or loss from business operations. This is done by deducting administration, financial and selling and distribution overheads from the gross profit, derived from the trading account, adding any income from investments and subtracting financial charges such as bank interest.

Profit to sales ratio. The profit before tax expressed as a percentage of sales value.

Programme evaluation and review technique (PERT). *See* CRITICAL PATH ANALYSIS.

Project control. 1. A procedure for controlling the expenditure incurred on capital projects. When projects have been approved the relevant contracts are negotiated and each project is allocated a number for identification purposes and for the cost finding and recording. Details of expenditure commitments and actual expenditure are recorded on a project control sheet. The control sheet is monitored to detect any overspending and the need for supplementary expenditure approvals. 2. The term may also relate to the use of network analysis (q.v.), critical path method (CPM) (q.v.) and programme evaluation and review technique (PERT) (q.v.), for the planning and control of complex projects.

Project management. The planning and control of projects undertaken in a business from their initial inception to final completion. This embraces the management of the resources being used including the control of expenditure and the time span for performing tasks. The project manager is normally in charge of a project team.

Projects committee. A committee formed for the purpose of establishing the economic viability of projects, i.e. benefits and cost effectiveness, comparison of alternative projects and determining the relative priority of projects under consideration, in order to allocate scarce resources to the most worthwhile projects.

Promotion. 1. The activity concerned with increasing sales volume. *See* SALES PROMOTION. 2. Appointing personnel to positions of greater responsibility and authority.

Public company. *See* COMPANY.

Public relations. A function concerned with promoting the image of a company to gain its acceptance by the public at large. It is concerned with projecting an acceptable image through acceptable public policies relating to employment, pollution of the environment, quality of its products, etc. It is a communications exercise via television, radio and the press. A company generates information to the media by way of press releases.

Purchasing. A function responsible for procuring all types of materials, parts and supplies for an organisation, ensuring they are ordered at the right time, received on the due date, accord with the level of quality required and that correct prices are charged. The function also establishes the economic order quantity (EOQ) (q.v.) for each item and determines stock control levels in liaison with the stock controller. Incoming invoices from suppliers are also checked against orders placed to ensure that the goods have been ordered and received. The values recorded on the invoices are also checked.

Purchasing budget. A budget which contains details of the materials and parts to be purchased to comply with the requirements of the production budget. It also contains the purchasing requirements of other functions including production and service departments in respect of maintenance materials, consumable supplies, etc.

Purchasing management. The purchasing function is usually the responsibility of the chief buyer or purchasing officer, who is responsible for controlling the ordering of materials of all types, rationalising the range of materials purchased in conjunction with the materials standards controller and design manager. Also responsible for providing reports regarding pending price changes and availability of new materials and the provision of price schedules to the management accountant for standard costing purposes where appropriate. Also oversees payments for purchases and that orders are effectively progressed.

Purpose organisation. *See* HETEROGENEOUS ORGANISATION STRUCTURE.

Pyramid structure. *See* ORGANISATION PYRAMID.

Q

Quality control. The function responsible for determining the quality standards of materials to be used in production, quality standards for manufactured and bought out parts and standards of finish and performance. Quality control ensures that the most suitable gauging and testing methods are employed and establishes quality control techniques such as statistical sampling (q.v.), using range and mean charts, spot checks, patrol viewing and acceptance sampling, etc.

Queueing theory. The name of a quantitative technique used for the analysis of business operations in which queues are involved. This may relate to queues of people at a bank teller position awaiting service either for paying in or for cashing a cheque; a supermarket where queues form at checkout points; people waiting for buses, etc. The technique involves the assessment of resources required to minimise the length of queue, by decreasing the average service time, perhaps by increasing the units of resources such as extra teller positions in a bank or supermarket checkout points. But the fact that there are periods when there are no queues at all when service facilities are idle, must be taken into account. The problem is to optimise service time, waiting or queueing time and the cost of resources.

Quorum. A term relevant to the conducting of management meetings and others of a similar nature. It is the minimum number of persons required to be in attendance in order to transact the business of a committee.

R

Rating. BS 3138:1979 defines the term "to rate" as follows: "To assess the worker's rate of working relative to the observer's concept of the rate corresponding to standard rating. The observer may take into account, separately or in combination, one or more factors necessary to the carrying out of the task, such as: speed of movement, effort, dexterity, consistency."

Redundancy. The term used to describe the situation when there is no work for the employees of a business and their employment is terminated.

Relationship, organisational. See EXECUTIVE, LATERAL RELATIONSHIPS and STAFF RELATIONSHIP.

Reorder level. The quantity of an item in stock which indicates it is necessary to place an order for its replenishment. The reorder level must provide for the time required for supplies to be received, i.e. the reorder period or lead time (q.v.), the usage during the reorder period and a safety stock to allow for variations in lead time and rate of usage.

Replacement of assets. See PLANT REPLACEMENT STRATEGY and ASSET REPLACEMENT.

Research and development strategy. A strategy which is essential for the future survival of a business. This strategy should include the need to pursue fundamental research to discover new knowledge and its assessment, by the process of applied research, into the ways of harnessing it to the products manufactured by the business. This should be followed by a strategy for development work. The strategy establishes the direction R & D will be undertaken in order to maintain a competitive position in the industry. It is essential to prepare a schedule of projects for the next five years, or other appropriate period, as a basis for monitoring progress. See also CORPORATE STRATEGY.

Reserves. See REVENUE RESERVE and CAPITAL RESERVES.

Resource planning. See PLANNING.

Responsibility accounting. See BUDGETARY CONTROL and ACCOUNTABILITY.

Responsibility, principle of. See ACCOUNTABILITY and PRINCIPLE OF RESPONSIBILITY.

Retail management. Managing the use of resources in a retail environment in the most effective way in order to achieve the desired level of customer satisfaction and profitability.

Return on capital employed (ROCE). This is a key ratio as it indicates the results achieved by the business, i.e. the profit earned in relation to the capital employed (q.v.) in earning it. The ratio may be computed as follows:

$$\frac{\text{Profit (before tax)} \times 100}{\text{Capital employed}}$$

Capital employed is usually the aggregate of share capital and reserves. See OBJECTIVE RATE OF RETURN.

Return on investment. See RETURN ON CAPITAL EMPLOYED.

Return on operating assets. See PRIMARY RATIO.

Revenue reserve. The setting aside of part of the revenue (income or profits) of a business, derived from the sale of goods or services, for the purpose of being self-financing to avoid high interest charges on bank loans.

Revenue reserves belong to the ordinary shareholders of the company.

Reward reviews. *See* APPRAISAL.

Risk analysis. *See* MAXIMAX RULE, MINIMAX RULE, DECISION THEORY and MAXIMUM LIKELIHOOD RULE.

Robotics. The use of robots for performing tasks previously performed by humans. They are used for automating or mechanising industrial processes and activities such as material handling. They may be defined as cybernetic devices having facilities for communicating and controlling their actions by means of programs. They have appropriate electronic sensory devices for observation, touch and for the application of pressure.

Role playing. *See* MANAGEMENT TRAINING TECHNIQUES.

S

Safety stock. A quantity of material or number of items retained in stock to provide for variations in usage and for the time lapse necessary to obtain new supplies, whether from external or internal sources.

Sales budget. A budget consisting of details of potential sales for a defined future period derived from the sales forecasts (q.v.). It contains details of products to be sold including quantities, selling prices and sales values. The data is used for monitoring actual results.

Sales forecast. An estimate of potential sales based on sales research for assessing the economic factors likely to prevail in the relevant forecasting period. Forecasting often utilises the technique of exponential smoothing (q.v.). *See* DEMAND FORECASTING.

Sales management. The activity controlled by the sales manager who is often responsible to the marketing manager. It is concerned with the control of selling activities, after-sales service, sales administration, warehousing, stock control and distribution.

Sales promotion. Promoting sales embraces all of the techniques available to sell more products or merchandise by means of direct representation, circulars, advertising in local and/or national newspapers or local and/or national television. Very often dealers in specific products, such as microcomputers, invite selected people or the public at large, to attend demonstrations of their equipment at local hotels.

Scalar principle. *See* CHAIN OF COMMAND.

Scientific approach to problem solving. *See* PROBLEM SOLVING.

Scientific management. *See* ORGANISATION THEORY 1 and PIONEERS OF MANAGEMENT.

Selection tests. These aim to provide an objective means of measuring individual abilities and/or characteristics. Tests involve the application of standard procedures to subjects which enable their responses to be quantified. The differences in the numerical scores represent differences in abilities or behaviour. The main types of tests used are: (*a*) intelligence tests which measure IQ; (*b*) aptitude and attainment tests which are designed to predict the potential an individual has to perform a job or specific tasks within a job; (*c*) personality tests which attempt to assess the type of personality possessed by the applicant. *See* APPRAISAL.

Self-development. *See* MANAGEMENT TRAINING TECHNIQUES.

Senior management. Managers in charge of line functions and service functions are classified as senior management. Examples include: works manager, marketing manager, chief designer, chief buyer, personnel manager, chief accountant, data processing manager and manager of management services.

Sensitivity analysis. *See* MODELLING PACKAGE.

Sensitivity training. *See* MANAGEMENT TRAINING TECHNIQUES.

Seven-point plan. The use of a check list when analysing jobs to assist in avoiding the omission of important factors. The checklist contains seven categories of analysis, hence the name. It was developed by Professor Alec Rodger. The plan analyses human attributes to determine the nature of the person required to perform a specific job as follows: (i) physical make-up, (ii) attainments, (iii) general intelligence, (iv) disposition, (v) specialised aptitudes, (vi) interests and (vii) circumstances.

Share capital. The number of shares that a limited company is authorised to issue is defined in the Memorandum of Association. It represents the capital of the business when the shares are taken up by shareholders, i.e. the issued capital which is converted into fixed and current assets such as plant and machinery and stocks of material, etc. for the pursuance of business operations. Shareholders are the owners of the business to the extent of the number of shares they hold. *See* CAPITAL.

Simplification. The process of simplifying tasks by the elimination of unnecessary complexity. This may be achieved, according to circumstances, in a number of ways: by reorganising the flow of work to eliminate unnecessary movement of personnel or materials; providing jigs to improve work handling e.g. for electroplated parts; separation of combined operations or the combination of separate operations, whichever suits the needs; changing the method, i.e. the type of machine or process. Products can also be simplified so that they are easier to manipulate and control, for example, motor car controls, microcomputers, washing machines, etc.

Simulation. The process of studying the behaviour of real-life systems by building a model containing all the relevant variables, constraints, and probabilities in the form of algorithms, etc. In some instances a system cannot be specified in precise algorithmic terms because it behaves in an unpredictable manner, i.e. it is a stochastic or probabilistic system (q.v.). It is then necessary to collect historical data or estimated values regarding frequencies and to apply Monte Carlo techniques (q.v.) to simulate the random behaviour of the system. Simulation programs run on a computer enable the real-life system to be studied over a number of years in a very short time, perhaps a matter of minutes or hours. Management is then provided with sufficient behavioural features of the system to use for the implementation of changes, to achieve the more efficient operation of an existing system, or the installation of a new system.

Site management. Concerned with the management of the resources to be used for a specific project at a particular location. This relates to the construction or maintenance of a section of motorway; construction of a factory estate, housing estate, new office block, bridge, etc. The site manager is responsible for hiring and firing casual manpower and for planning and progressing work and materials to ensure the project maintains its time and cost schedules in order to avoid penalties.

Source and disposition of funds statement. A statement constructed from the analysis of two balance sheets, one for the previous period and one relating to the current period, to assess the changes in assets and liabilities which have contributed to the difference in the cash balance or overdraft shown in the latest balance sheet. This may be set out in the following way:

	£	£
Disposition of funds:		
Fixed assets:		
Increase: Buildings	x	
Plant and machinery	x	
Other fixed assets	x	
		x

Investments:			
Increase: External investments		x	
Subsidiary companies		x	
			x
Current assets:			
Increase: Stocks		x	
Debtors		x	
			x
Increase in total assets			x

Source of funds:		
Increase: Creditors	x	
Accruals	x	
Provision for dividends	x	
Provision for corporation tax	x	
Issue of shares	x	
Sale of fixed assets	x	
	£	
Net profit	x	
Add depreciation	x	
		x
		x

Span of control. *See* PRINCIPLE OF THE SPAN OF CONTROL.

Specialisation. Relates to the division of labour and the use of special purpose machines and equipment. In a large organisation, personnel usually limit their activities to one main task, enabling them to become proficient and to increase productivity. This also applies to special purpose machines and processes. Specialisation also facilitates training, work allocation and job scheduling as well as more effective control. It is one of the three Ss, i.e. specialisation, standardisation and simplification. *See* FUNCTIONAL ORGANISATION and ORGANISATION PRINCIPLES.

Staffing. This element of management provides a business with manpower resources for its various activities. A formal staffing policy provides for management succession planning (q.v.) at all levels in the organisation. Effective staffing needs to be supported by an adequate training and development scheme.

Staff relationship. Non-executive relationships whereby personnel act in an advisory capacity, examples being internal auditors, O & M staff and other management services personnel, as well as committees such as those relating to works safety and data processing. They do not have authority to implement change in most instances, but can only make recommendations. *See* LINE AND STAFF ORGANISATION.

Staff suggestion scheme. A scheme which allows personnel, both in the factory and administrative functions, to make suggestions for simplifying work, improving methods of doing work or elimination of unnecessary work. Suggestions are reviewed by a committee and those which can be adopted are implemented and the relevant persons are rewarded. The value of the reward is related to the value of the suggestion to the business.

Standard. A standard may be defined as a yardstick consisting of a specific set of factors, relating to a particular entity, which may be in the form of a specification or a measurable quantity to provide guidelines for acceptable levels of quality, cost, performance, manufacturing specifications, etc. There exists many British Standards relating to forms and paper sizes, screw sizes, electrical and building standards. Attempts are also being made to standardise terminology relating to management accounting and data processing.

Standard cost. The Institute of Cost and Management Accountants define standard cost as "A predetermined calculation of how much costs should be under specified working conditions. It is built up from an assessment of the value of cost elements and correlates technical specifications and the quantification of materials, labour and other costs to the prices and/or wage rates expected to apply during the period in which the standard cost is intended to be used. Its main purposes are to provide bases for control through variance accounting (q.v.), for the valuation of stock and work in progress and, in some cases, for fixing selling prices."

Standard costing. A costing technique which uses predetermined costs, i.e. standard costs and predetermined selling prices, as a basis of control by analysing variances between standard and actual results. *See also* COST ACCOUNTING.

Standard deviation. The mathematical formula for the normal curve contains an element for measuring dispersion of variables from an average or mean value, in order to establish the variability of data in precise terms. This is known as the standard deviation and has the symbol σ. There is a direct relationship with regard to the proportion of the total number of items (statistically referred to as the population) which is measured by the number of standard deviations from the mean. The total area of a normal curve contains the total population, i.e. all the items of a frequency distribution (q.v.). The most widely used measures of dispersion are:

Number of items contained in defined areas of the normal curve (%)	Standard deviations either side of the mean
68.0	1.0
95.0	2.0
99.0	2.5
99.7	3.0

The characteristics outlined above provide a method of establishing a measure of probability for a stated level of confidence. For instance, there is a 68 per cent probability of the lead time for replenishing stock being within ± one standard deviation of the average lead time. Similarly, there is a 95 per cent probability of customer demand being within two standard deviations of the average quantity required. *See* NORMAL DISTRIBUTION.

Standard hour. *See* STANDARD PERFORMANCE.

Standardisation. Standardisation is a means of achieving economy of production by concentrating on a limited number of products or manufacturing a range of products which are assembled from standard parts. This type of standardisation also achieves economy in design and development costs, the cost of tooling and packaging. The range of parts and materials in the stores is also reduced thereby optimising the investment in stocks. Specifications of many products are contained in British Standards in respect of electrical goods, screw threads, sizes, etc. One of the three Ss of industry, the others being simplification (q.v.) and specialisation (q.v.).

Standard performance. BS 3138:1979 defines standard performance as: "The rate of output which qualified workers can achieve without overexertion as an average over the working day or shift provided they adhere to the specified method and provided they are motivated to apply themselves to their work. This is represented by 100 on the BS scale." (This corresponds to the production of 1 standard hour of work per hour or 60 standard minutes per 60 minutes.)

Standard rating. BS 3138:1979 defines this as "The rating corresponding to the average rate at which qualified workers will naturally work, provided that they adhere to the specified method and that they are motivated to apply themselves to their work. If the standard rating is consistently maintained and the appropriate relaxation is taken, a qualified worker will achieve standard performance over the working day or shift."

Statistical sampling. A technique for establishing the characteristics of the whole of a population by means of samples established statistically. Used for quality control and market research and for establishing the work pattern of a department by means of activity sampling (q.v.). Statistical quality control charts have outer and inner control limits which indicate statistical control limits. If the number of errors are outside the statistical expectation the process is stopped in order to detect the assignable cause.

Statistical stock control. This is the assessment of statistical variability of supply and demand in order to optimise capital invested in stocks related to the level of service provided. *See* STANDARD DEVIATION.

Stochastic system. The state of a system whose behaviour varies in a random manner as a result of environmental influences is difficult to predict. Recourse must therefore be had to assessing the probable outputs or state of affairs on a probability basis, using historical data for the preparation of frequency distributions in order to compute standard deviations for various degrees of confidence. *See* PROBABILISTIC SYSTEM and STANDARD DEVIATION.

Stock audit. A stock audit is for the purpose of establishing that the physical stock of items held in the stores corresponds with that recorded in stores records. Any differences are investigated and recorded on a stock audit report to enable the stores records to be adjusted. Serious discrepancies are reported to the appropriate manager as it is possible for stocks to be misappropriated. A number of methods may be adopted for checking stocks, e.g. auditing major items regularly, checking a number of items each day to ensure that all stocks are checked perhaps twice during the course of a year, checking each item when the reorder level is reached thereby minimising the quantity to be checked either by counting, weighing, measurement or sampling methods. The audit is also concerned with ensuring that all stock movements are accurately recorded, that correct prices are used for stock evaluations, for assessing the extent of stock losses by faulty handling, pilferage, faulty booking and also ensuring that adequate control is applied to minimise capital locked up in stocks. Auditing also checks that replenishment orders are placed when stocks reach the reorder level, assesses stock obsolescence, and the extent of stock deterioration.

Stock control. Stocks form a buffer to facilitate variations in supply and demand and act as a reservoir which is topped up by incoming supplies and which is drained by outflows to production. Very often stocks constitute a high proportion of current assets and, of course, working capital, and they must be controlled in the most suitable way to ensure they do not exceed an optimum level. Stock control is achieved by the recording of all stock movements in and out of the stores which includes receipts from suppliers, issues to production, returns to stores, returns to supplier, stock reserves and adjustments as a result of stock auditing. Control is also implemented by means of stock control parameters including safety stock (q.v.) level, maximum stock level and the level at which stocks should be replenished, that is the reorder level. Supplies are often obtained on the basis of economic order quantity (EOQ) (q.v.) for stock optimisation purposes.

Stock controller. Responsible for the day-to-day control of stocks by means of perpetual inventory control records and ensuring that stock items are replenished in accordance with the predetermined reorder level and economic order quantity (q.v.). Provides reports in respect of stock losses, shortages, dormant, obsolete and free stocks to the chief buyer and production manager. Also provides details of issues to production and quantities in stock to the management accountant for the preparation of periodic operating reports and balance sheets.

Stock management. *See* STOCK CONTROLLER.

Stock turnover ratio. A ratio for indicating the number of times per year the stock is turned over. The more rapid the turnover, the greater the efficiency of stock management and the business as a whole. A rapid turnover indicates that surplus stocks are not being held, but if the turnover is too rapid, due perhaps to increasing demand or a too low level of stocks, then there is a danger of a high frequency of stock shortages. The ratio may be computed by two methods.

Method 1. Stock turnover ratio =
$$\frac{\text{Cost of goods sold (for the year)}}{\text{Average stock (at cost)}}$$

Method 2. Stock turnover ratio =
$$\frac{\text{Sales (for the year)}}{\text{Average stock (at cost)}}$$

Storage time ratio. A ratio which is used to indicate the number of days' or weeks' consumption represented by the stock-holding of raw materials and component parts and the number of days' or weeks' sales represented by the stocks of finished goods. In addition, the ratio may be used to inform management of the number of days' or weeks' sales represented by work-in-progress. The ratio may be calculated in two ways.

Method 1. Storage time in weeks =
$$\frac{52 \text{ (weeks in the year)}}{\text{Stock turnover rate}}$$
(*See* STOCK TURNOVER RATIO)

Method 2. Storage time in weeks =
$$\frac{\text{Average stock (at cost)} \times 52}{\text{Sales (for year)}}$$

Stores audit. *See* STOCK AUDIT.

Strategic gap. When developing corporate plans the difference between what a business wants to achieve and what it is likely to achieve, unless some action is taken to improve the prospective future situation, is known as the strategic gap. The gap may be attributable to anticipated sales volumes being lower than in the past, which may be attributable to products reaching the later stages of their life cycles, or because plant and machinery is technologically obsolete and is unable to achieve the required volume of production efficiently and economically. The strategy to be applied to close the gap may be the introduction of new products before the end of the life cycles of the current products, to penetrate new markets, to increase selling prices, to automate the manufacturing processes or whatever seems appropriate in the circumstances.

Strategic planning. Strategic planning is an activity concerned with determining suitable strategies for increasing the profitability and survival of a business. This is the province of corporate planning which defines the objectives to be achieved in the long term and establishes the strategies to be employed to achieve them within the framework of corporate policy. Various strategies may be adopted either singly or in combination. They include product-market strategy (q.v.), diversification strategy (q.v.), divestment strategy (q.v.), horizontal integration (q.v.) and vertical integration strategies (q.v.), distribution strategy, technological strategy, financial strategy, managerial strategy, research and development strategy, product design strategy, cost reduction strategy, etc.

Strategy development. *See* DEVELOPMENT OF STRATEGY.

Strike. The withdrawal of services by the employees of a business due to an unresolved dispute between the workers' union and the management of the business. The leaders of the relevant union usually call for the strike in an attempt to resolve the conflict when negotiations have broken down.

Structured decisions. The rules governing some types of decisions may be formulated in mathematical or statistical algorithms. Decisions of this type are classed as routine or structured decisions. A notable example is stock control regarding stock replenishments. When stock items reach a predefined reorder level the items are ordered on the basis of comparing the quantity in stock with the reorder level and if the quantity is equal to or less than the reorder level the item is reordered. This type of decision can be automated as the algorithms can be built into a computer program and the items to be replenished are printed out on an exception report. This is accomplished by a branching routine in the program. *See* AUTOMATED DECISIONS.

Sub-objectives. Sub-objectives are objectives which are subsidiary to the primary objective. For example, the primary objective of a factory may be to reduce production costs in a number of ways. Accordingly sub-objectives may be defined in the following terms: increase machine utilisation by 5 per cent to 85 per cent; reduce idle time from 2 per cent to 1 per cent of total production time; reduce labour turnover from 15 per cent to 5 per cent; increase operator performance to an average of 120 per cent from present 110 per cent; reduce scrap rate to 5 per cent of good production from present 8 per cent.

Subsidiary budget. Subsidiary budgets are the individual budgets which when combined form the master budget (q.v.). They include the sales budget, production budget, purchases budget, plant and machinery budget, capital expenditure budget, manpower budget, cash budget, etc.

Sub-system. A sub-system may be defined as a system which when combined with other sub-systems forms a larger system; it may therefore be described as an element of a larger system. For example, the production system is a sub-system within the environment of a total system consisting of integrated physical and control systems. The production sub-system itself consists of smaller sub-systems in the form of machines (mechanical sub-systems) which are also interrelated with the machines' operators (human sub-systems who may be classified as unique self-adapting systems). In addition, there exist work handling sub-systems, either human or automatic, and the power supply sub-system all of which interact with each other to form the hub of business operations. Physical sub-systems are governed by control sub-systems and the information required for control is generated by separately structured data processing (information systems) sub-systems.

Sub-system objectives. From a business organisation point of view a department may be defined as a sub-system which functions within the framework of a larger sub-system, i.e. a function. Individual departments (sub-systems) are set objectives within the framework of functional objectives and accordingly they may be defined as sub-objectives (q.v.).

Supervisory management. Supervisory managers are usually managers of sections within a department, consisting of a number of groups of personnel each responsible to a group leader. Supervisory managers are in an intermediary position between departmental managers and group leaders. Within factory departments, supervisory managers are normally called foremen and in the larger office they may have the title of section leader. In general, they are responsible for controlling the activities of group leaders, implementing instructions from their departmental manager, allocating work to groups and coordinating the activities of the groups to achieve the common objective. In addition, the senior section leader or foreman may deputise for the departmental manager. Examples of this class of supervisory management include: production foreman, maintenance foreman, inspection foreman, transport supervisor, warehouse supervisor, typing and reprographics supervisor, budgetary control supervisor, cost accounting supervisor, cashier, shift leader (computer department), project leaders, etc.

Synergy. The concept that the output of an organisation may differ in quantity and quality from the sum of the inputs is referred to as synergy or the synergistic effect. In ordinary arithmetic $2 + 2 = 4$. However, in "organisational" arithmetic 2 units of input + 2 more units of input may give 3, 4, 7, 13, A, X, or Z units of output. The units of output may be the same dimension as the input units and may be equal to or different from their arithmetic sum as 3, 4, 7 and 13. Output 3 represents an unsuccessful organisation, output 4 is a break-even one and 7 and 13 represent successful organisations as their output is greater than their costs or inputs. Outputs A, X and Z are representative of the fact that the dimension of output may be qualitatively different from input units.

System. A system may be defined as a combination of interrelated elements, or sub-systems (q.v.), organised in such a way as to ensure the efficient functioning of the system as a whole. This necessitates a high degree of coordination between the sub-systems, each of which is designed to achieve a specified purpose. This may be compared with the organisation of a business which is structured on the basis of functions, each of which may be classed as a sub-system. Each function must operate within the framework of corporate objectives, i.e. of the total system. The functional activities are controlled by a functional manager and the managing director acts as the chief coordinator.

Systems approach. *See* ORGANISATION THEORY 4 and PIONEERS OF MANAGEMENT.

T

Tactical planning. This type of planning is concerned with preparing plans for the achievement of the strategic plan. Factors to consider include the planning of an effective organisation structure, product-market development (q.v.), resource development and capital planning. Primarily, tactical planning is concerned with the way in which strategic objectives can best be achieved, i.e. the tactics to be employed.

Tactics. See TACTICAL PLANNING.

Takeover bid. A bid by one company to acquire sufficient shares in another to obtain a controlling interest. A pending takeover bid often causes the market price of shares to rise.

Tangible assets. Assets of substance. See FIXED ASSETS.

Taylor, F.W. (1856–1915). See ORGANISATION THEORY 1 and PIONEERS OF MANAGEMENT.

Team management. See PROJECT MANAGEMENT, MANAGING DIRECTOR and TOP MANAGEMENT.

Technological strategy. Consumers generally require products incorporating the latest technology and accordingly a business must respond to this to maintain or increase its share of the market. The silicon chip has created what one may call a second industrial revolution because many manufacturers are now incorporating microprocessors produced from silicon chips into their products. Electronic toys and games incorporate them as do word processors and microcomputers, electric cookers, washing machines, pocket calculators and digital watches. Motor cars incorporate small computers for monitoring petrol consumption. Such developments require a company to have a forward-looking approach to technological innovation to keep abreast of the forever shifting scene. See also CORPORATE STRATEGY.

Teletext. A generic term for textual information displayed on a television screen which is broadcast by a television company. It includes *Ceefax*—the teletext system transmitted by the BBC—and *Oracle*—the teletext system transmitted by the IBA. Prestel is not broadcast by a television company as the users' Prestel television is connected to a telephone line which links it to the Prestel computer. See INFORMATION TECHNOLOGY and PRESTEL.

Terotechnology. The technology of care from the Greek "térein". It is concerned with economic life cycle costs of business assets (plant and machinery) balanced against the resources used throughout their life. It relates to the effective management of physical assets embracing engineering maintenance, the cost of financial resources used in maintaining plant and buildings in good working order, performance statistics and the continual feedback of information to management so that balanced decisions can be made either to continue to maintain plant or to replace it with plant of more modern design and improved productivity. It is also concerned with buildings and other structures as well as plant and machinery.

T groups. See MANAGEMENT TRAINING TECHNIQUES.

Theory X. A theory relating to human behaviour in the working environment. This particular theory assumes that the average human being dislikes work of any kind and will avoid it whenever possible. Because of this human characteristic, the theory implies that people must be ordered, directed or enforced to work at a reasonable level of performance to allow business objectives to be accomplished. This situation necessitates strict discipline and supervision. The theory declares that workers tend to be shy of accepting responsibility. *See* MOTIVATION THEORY.

Theory Y. A theory of human behaviour which assumes that people prefer to work and that the mental and physical effort expended in such an activity is as natural as that applied to other activities, such as leisure pursuits. People achieve self-satisfaction from the application of initiative and do not need strict supervision in order to pursue the goals set for them. Workers tend not only to accept responsibility but also to seek it. *See* MOTIVATION THEORY.

Therblig. The name given to work elements contained in the various tasks performed by workers. The term "Therblig" is a reversal of the name "Gilbreth", i.e. Frank B. Gilbreth who was initially responsible for analysing tasks into fundamental work elements. These include search, find, select, grasp, hold, transport, load, position, assemble, etc. Therbligs are used for conducting methods studies, each Therblig having a unique symbol and colour.

Thinktank. A name given to a group of experts from a number of fields who get together for the purpose of combining their knowledge and experience in order to solve complex problems. The technique may be used for the solution of operational research problems as each expert views the problem from a different point of view, enabling a variety of approaches to be made. What may seem to be a personnel problem may in fact be one of ergonomics, plant layout, methods, work simplification or a psychological problem. An accountant tends to view a problem from a financial viewpoint whereas an engineer will appraise a problem from an engineering standpoint. *See also* BRAINSTORMING.

Threats. Business is conducted in an environment largely hostile, containing more threats than opportunities, highlighted at present by the number of businesses which have gone into liquidation or which are closing down part of their operations. Most threats are of an economic nature, heightened by the world-wide recession, causing high unemployment and tending to reduce demand, particularly of luxury goods causing further unemployment. Added to this is the scourge of inflation, which although not so high now, nevertheless remains a threat. Excessive inflation is partly caused by pay demands outstripping increases in productivity. The threat of competition is also high, particularly to manufacturers in the UK of such products as hi-fi, TV, videos, motor cars and motor cycles, both from Europe and the Far East.

Three Ss. *See* SPECIALISATION, STANDARDISATION, and SIMPLIFICATION.

Time study. Time study using a stopwatch is defined by BS 3138:1979 as "A work measurement technique designed to establish the time for a qualified worker to carry out specified elements under specified conditions at a defined rate of working, recorded by direct observation of the times, using a time measuring device and the ratings for individual elements." The method used for timing will depend on the volume and frequency of the task, the cycle time of the operation and the cost of conducting the measurement programme. For extreme accuracy of timing a stop-watch should be used to measure each element. In many office situations sufficient accuracy may be obtained by the use of the office clock or a wrist-watch. *See* RATING.

Top management. This consists of the functional managers of a business, also known as senior executives. The functional managers as a whole form the management team of which the managing director is the team leader. The functional managers interpret the instructions issued to them by the chief executive and convert them into detailed plans for implementation. They are accountable for the achievement of the objectives for which they have delegated responsibility and authority.

Total systems approach. An approach to systems development which recognises that all systems within a business are related to each other to a greater, or lesser, extent. This must be so because a business as a whole is a complete system, i.e. a total system, comprising all the functional systems which support the individual functions. The "total systems approach" recognises the relationships and interdependence of systems. This approach enables a number of related sub-systems to be integrated to form a larger system. For example, an integrated order-entry system provides for data validation, credit control, stock control, invoicing and sales ledger accounting routines. The input to the system (details of customers order requirements) triggers off the other sub-systems, which are highly related to each other, as an item shipped to a customer affects not only the stock position but also warehouse despatching. This in turn generates an invoice for the goods despatched which are recorded in the sales ledger against the customers account, and so on. This integrated system offers a number of advantages, e.g. with regard to an integrated computer system, data are entered as input to a system only once and all relevant records are updated automatically. By this means data can be retrieved according to functional needs, especially if the integrated system is supported by a database. The total systems approach requires a detailed analysis of all business systems in order to define the relationships between inputs, files and outputs as well as types of information and the frequency with which it is required by specific managers for control and decision-making purposes. *See* ORGANISATION THEORY 4.

Trading account. A summary of the purchases and sales of a business or the production cost of goods sold and the value of sales. The difference between the elements establishes the gross profit or loss which is then carried forward to the profit and loss account for determining the net profit or loss after deducting administration, selling and distribution overheads.

Trading certificate. A document issued by the Registrar of companies which provides a company with the authority to commence trading.

Trading profit. *See* OPERATING PROFIT.

Training. *See* MANAGEMENT DEVELOPMENT.

Transactional analysis. *See* MANAGEMENT TRAINING TECHNIQUES.

"Two Factor Theory". *See* MOTIVATION THEORY 2.

U

Undercapitalised. The situation which relates to a business with insufficient capital for the level of business being undertaken. This causes cash flow problems which makes it necessary to finance business operations by bank loans or overdrafts at high rates of interest. The remedy is to increase the authorised capital and issued capital. If the issued capital is less than the authorised capital then the unissued capital can be issued, or uncalled capital called in. *See* OVER-CAPITALISATION.

Uneconomic. An undertaking, such as a proposed project, which is not a viable proposition in terms of anticipated benefits related to the cost of achieving them.

Unfair dismissal. A manager should be aware of what constitutes unfair dismissal, particularly those managers having responsibility for hiring and firing. An employee has the right to bring an action for unfair dismissal under s. 54 of the Employment Protection Consolidation Act 1978. An employer can show dismissal was fair if it accords to s. 57 of that act, i.e. (*i*) dismissal was based on employee's lack of ability; (*ii*) dismissal was based on employee's lack of qualifications; (*iii*) dismissal was based on employee's conduct; (*iv*) employee was fairly selected for redundancy; (*v*) it would be a criminal offence to continue to employ the person concerned; (*vi*) any other substantial reason. When the employer has shown one of the above, the tribunal must decide if the employer acted reasonably in treating the reason as a sufficient reason to justify dismissal. The tribunal can find dismissal to be unfair but that the employee contributed towards it and reduce damages accordingly.

Uniform costing. A standardised costing technique which can be applied to any method of costing whether it is job, process, contract or operation. It may be adopted by several companies in a group or related industry to facilitate cost comparisons for relative measures of performance. It involves the use of standardised cost codes, cost structures (elements of cost), methods of recording costing data and the method of absorbing general overheads. *See also* COST ACCOUNTING.

Unit cost. The cost of producing one unit of a product. This may be on the basis of marginal cost (q.v.) or total cost, i.e. absorption costing (q.v.). Marginal costing only takes account of variable costs and the cost remains constant regardless of the volume of production, i.e. level of activity. On the other hand, when applying absorption costing the cost of each unit of product contains a portion of general overheads some of which are fixed regardless of changes in the level of activity; consequently the unit cost varies inversely with level of activity. *See also* FIXED COSTS.

Unity of command. *See* CHAIN OF COMMAND.

Unity of direction. All business functions must pursue a common direction for the attainment of corporate objectives. This is accomplished by the board of directors establishing objectives for each function within the framework of corporate goals. The managing director then implements these requirements and monitors the achievements of each function to ensure they accord with pre-determined objectives.

Unity of objective. *See* OBJECTIVES.

Universalist theory. *See* DIRECTING.

Unlimited liability. Shareholders, the owners of a company, are responsible for the whole of the debts of a business organised on an unlimited liability basis. *See* COMPANY and LIMITED LIABILITY.

Unrealised profit. *See* PAPER PROFIT.

Utilisation of assets. *See* ASSET UTILISATION RATIO.

Utilisation ratio. *See* ASSET UTILISATION RATIO.

V

Value added. The increase in value of a product as a consequence of additional processing operations, the cost of which represents the additional value. Added value also occurs when transportation costs are added to the value of goods when they are transferred from a factory or warehouse to sales outlets. The cost of materials purchased does not form part of added value to the purchaser but amounts added for profit margins are included. *See* ADDED VALUE.

Value analysis. An activity which is concerned with establishing whether all the parts contained in a product have a value commensurate with its cost. Very often parts are too complex for their functional purpose and consequently cost more than they need to. When the parts are simplified they can be produced at much lower cost and have a satisfactory cost/value ratio. Sometimes parts can be made from less expensive material without impairing safety, quality or performance. The design of a product needs periodic review to ensure that it is the best for current circumstances, including the current state of technology. Value analysis has a high pay-off when mass production is paramount, as small savings on the cost of manufacture of each part or product can generate major savings in total.

Variable costs. These are costs directly associated with the product, i.e. direct labour for converting direct material into the required form, and the variable overheads which can be allocated to the product. Such costs vary in total in direct proportion to the level of activity but remain constant per unit produced. *See* UNIT COST and CONTRIBUTION.

Variable overheads. Overhead expenses which can be directly identified to a specific product and which remain constant per unit of output regardless of the level of activity attained. Such costs form part of marginal cost (q.v.).

Variance. *See* COST VARIANCE.

Variance accounting. Budgetary control (q.v.) and standard costing (q.v.) systems incorporate variance accounting as they are concerned with the difference between budgets/standards and the actual results achieved. The differences are referred to as variances which are computed from accounting procedures; hence, variance accounting or accounting for variances. The variances are used for the preparation of exception reports to facilitate the technique of management by exception (q.v.). *See* EXCEPTION REPORTING.

Variety reduction. *See* STANDARDISATION.

Venture capital. Some banks have entered the venture capital market for the provision of what is known as equity capital for financing proposed ventures considered commercially viable. The term venture capital often refers to the capital and management assistance provided by a specialist investment capital company for creating a new business, or for specific ventures to be undertaken by existing businesses.

Vertical integration. The process of consolidation whereby a business diversifies its activities either backwards towards the supply of essential materials or forwards to sales outlets. It may elect to manufacture its own materials for the purpose of safeguarding continuity of supply. With regard to sales, a business may wish to have a greater degree of control of its sales and profits and decide to develop its own sales outlets. This integration is referred to as vertical as the business is either moving backwards or forwards vertically expanding the nature of its operations. This may also be achieved by takeovers.

Vertical organisation structure. *See* HETEROGENEOUS ORGANISATION STRUCTURE.

Vertical thinking. *See* LATERAL THINKING.

Vroom, V. *See* MOTIVATION THEORY 5.

W

What if? facilities. *See* MODELLING PACKAGE.

Woodward, Joan (1916–71). *See* PIONEERS OF MANAGEMENT.

Worker co-operatives. The co-operative idea has its roots in the social philosophies of Robert Owen and Philippe Buchez who maintained that the efforts of any commercial enterprise can be oriented towards the enrichment of investors, workers, and the community at large. There are consumer co-operatives—probably the best known example being the original Co-operative Wholesale Society—and producer co-operatives. It is the latter to which most people refer when discussing worker co-operatives and there are four main groups in Britain.

1. Old producer co-operatives which have survived from the early pioneering endeavours of the nineteenth century. While structures vary ownership is typically vested in "members" of the co-operative who may or may not be workers. Ownership and control is not primarily vested in the workforce.

2. The grouping of small common ownership enterprises known as ICOM (Industrial Common Ownership Movement). ICOM evolved from the iniatives of E. Bader. Stimulus for common ownership of individual firms has generally come from management. They have adopted the principle of collective ownership which means that the company's assets are owned by the entire workforce as a group. They have mainly been formed from existing private companies.

3. Worker takeovers promoted by Anthony Wedgwood Benn as Industry Secretary in the early 1970s. The highly publicised trio of Scottish Daily News, Meriden and Kirkby Manufacturing were converted to worker co-operatives from existing companies by the injection of substantial government money with the prime purpose of saving jobs.

4. Worker co-operatives which have adopted the individual ownership principle utilised by perhaps the most famous co-operative at Mondragon in the Basque region of Spain. Up to 70 per cent of all reinvestment is credited to the ownership of individual workers and they are paid out in full when they leave.

Worker takeovers. *See* WORKER CO-OPERATIVES.

Working capital. *See* NET CURRENT ASSETS.

Work measurement. *See* TIME STUDY.

Work scheduling. *See* PRODUCTION PLANNING AND CONTROL.

Works committee. *See* COMMITTEE.

Work-sharing. The EEC in their paper on work-sharing state that the general objective of work-sharing is to "redistribute the total volume of work in the economy in order to increase employment opportunities for all those wishing to work". Pressure for detailed consideration and implementation of work-sharing and its inclusion as one element within an overall economic strategy is emanating from many sources.

Work-sharing schemes may be divided into two main groups: First there are measures to reduce the time spent at work by the existing employed labour force. These include a reduction in the standard working week, reductions in overtime, increased annual holidays, extension of flexible working, increased part-time working and job sharing schemes. Secondly there are measures to reduce the number of people actively participating in the labour market, including early retirement, a longer period spent in education and training and periodic sabbaticals or study leaves.

Work simplification. *See* SIMPLIFICATION.

Works management. Responsible for ensuring that the planned level of production is achieved at the right time, at the right level of quality, at the right cost with a minimum of plant breakdowns and delays from other causes. In a medium to large manufacturing business, a works manager would generally report to the managing director or general manager. His subordinates would include the production manager, production controller, quality controller, works engineer and internal transport manager. In some instances the stock controller (q.v.) may be responsible to the works manager. The works manager may also be responsible for work study (q.v.).

Work study. An activity which embraces both method study and work measurement. It is usual to ensure that the best method is being applied to a task before establishing the time required to do it by some form of work measurement technique. *See* TIME STUDY and METHOD STUDY.

Work-to-rule. The practice of stringently observing rules and regulations governing the performance of specific activities. This has the effect of slowing down the rate of production, or the provision of services, entered into deliberately by the workforce in an attempt to resolve a dispute with management. If the action is unsuccessful a strike may be called.

Wrongful dismissal. *See* UNFAIR DISMISSAL.

YZ

Yield on investment. A technique of investment appraisal which avoids the arbitrary choice of a rate of interest when evaluating alternative investments. The procedure is to compute a rate of interest which will equate the present value of cash flows or cost savings with the present value of the cash outflows. The interest rate is found by trial and error and is known as the yield on investment. *See also* CAPITAL EXPENDITURE CONTROL.

Youth employment/unemployment. The Manpower Services Commission's statistics show that unemployment among young people (16 and 17 year olds) rose by 400 per cent between 1972 and 1980 and that they form a significant proportion of the total number of unemployed. In an attempt to combat this successive governments have introduced a variety of schemes including labour subsidies paid by the government to employers, vocational training, work experience programmes, work preparation schemes and college training under the Youth Training Scheme (YTS).

Zero base budgeting. This is defined by the ICMA as "A method of budgeting whereby all activities are re-evaluated each time a budget is formulated. Each functional budget starts with the assumption that the function does not exist and is at zero cost. Increments of cost are compared with increments of benefit, culminating in the planned maximum benefit for a given budgeted cost."

Zero-based administration. The concept of zero-based administration was developed by W.D. Scott, the international management consultants. It is a critical and fundamental analysis of functions, procedures, information and organisation. The zero-based approach demands that a company goes back to basics and establishes answers to two key questions: What are the real objectives of the business, the division or the function? What is the minimum administrative infrastructure required to satisfy these objectives? ZBA involves the evaluation of each major administrative activity against the criteria of relevance to the business and "value for money". As a result, the inessential, marginal and "nice to have" activities are identified and removed, resulting in a slimmer, more responsive and more effective administration.